What Makes Girls Sick and Tired

Lucile de Pesloüan • Geneviève Darling

Translated by Emma Rodgers with Myra Leibu

For
Shushanna Bikini London
L.P.

For Mel,
for your friendship
which always makes
me stronger #bff
G.D.

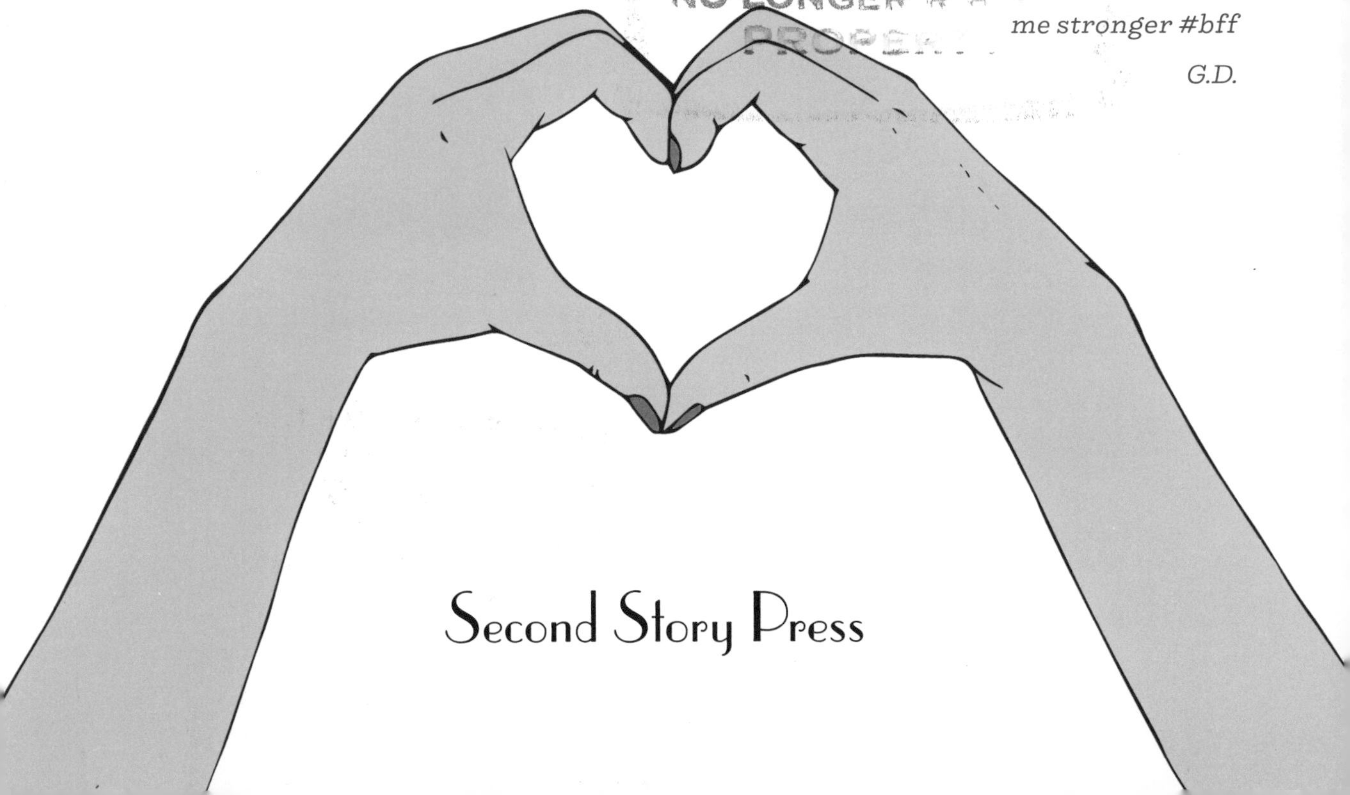

Second Story Press

Girls are sick and tired because sexism affects everyone, every day, in ways that are both obvious and subtle, and both simple and complex.

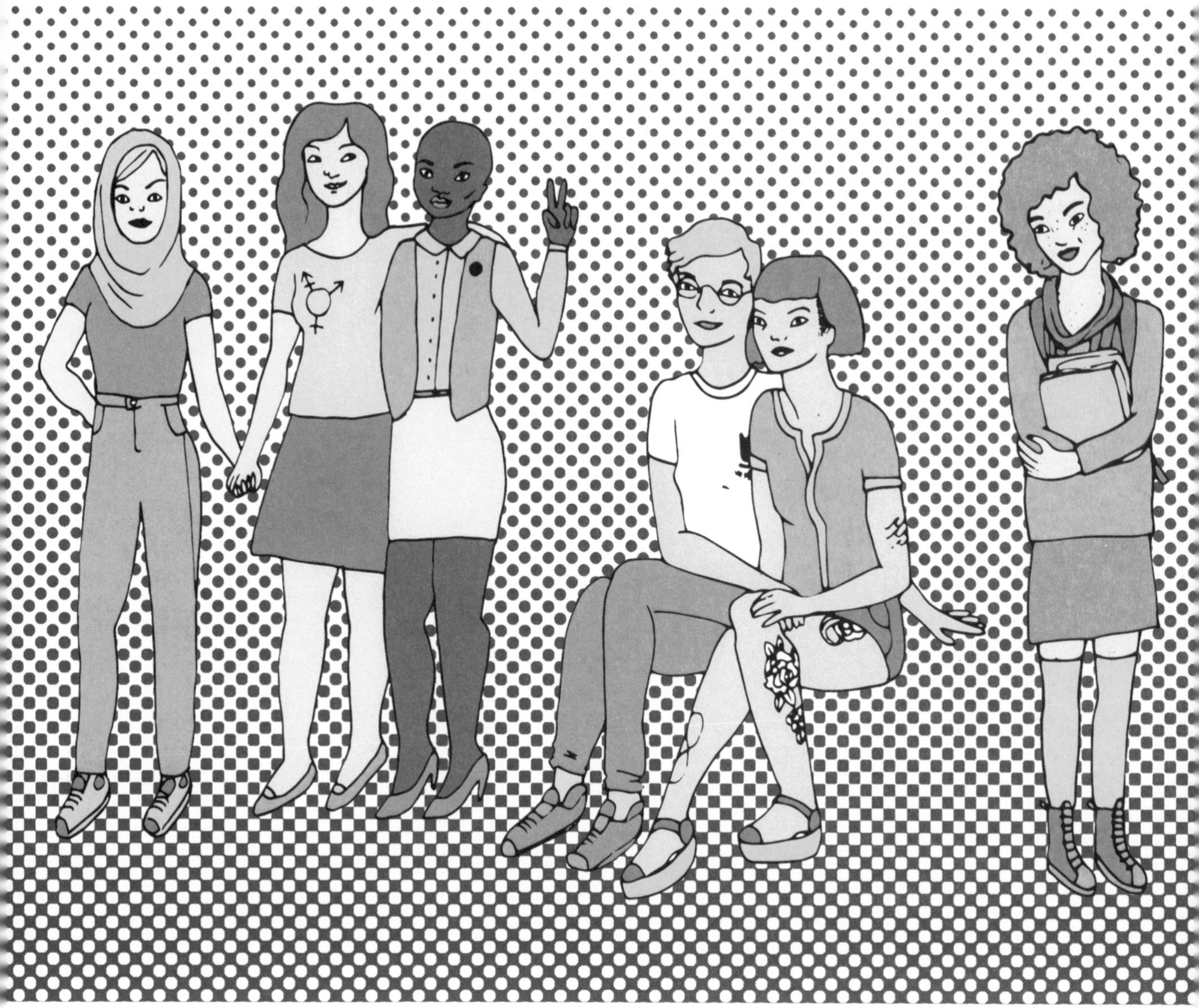

Girls live a wide range of experiences: there are gay girls, trans girls, queer girls, Indigenous girls, sad girls, sick girls, girls who are rich, who are poor, girls who are immigrants, racialized girls, white girls, city girls, suburban girls and country girls, girls with disabilities, tall girls and short girls, vegan girls, girls who are militant, confident, or shy...

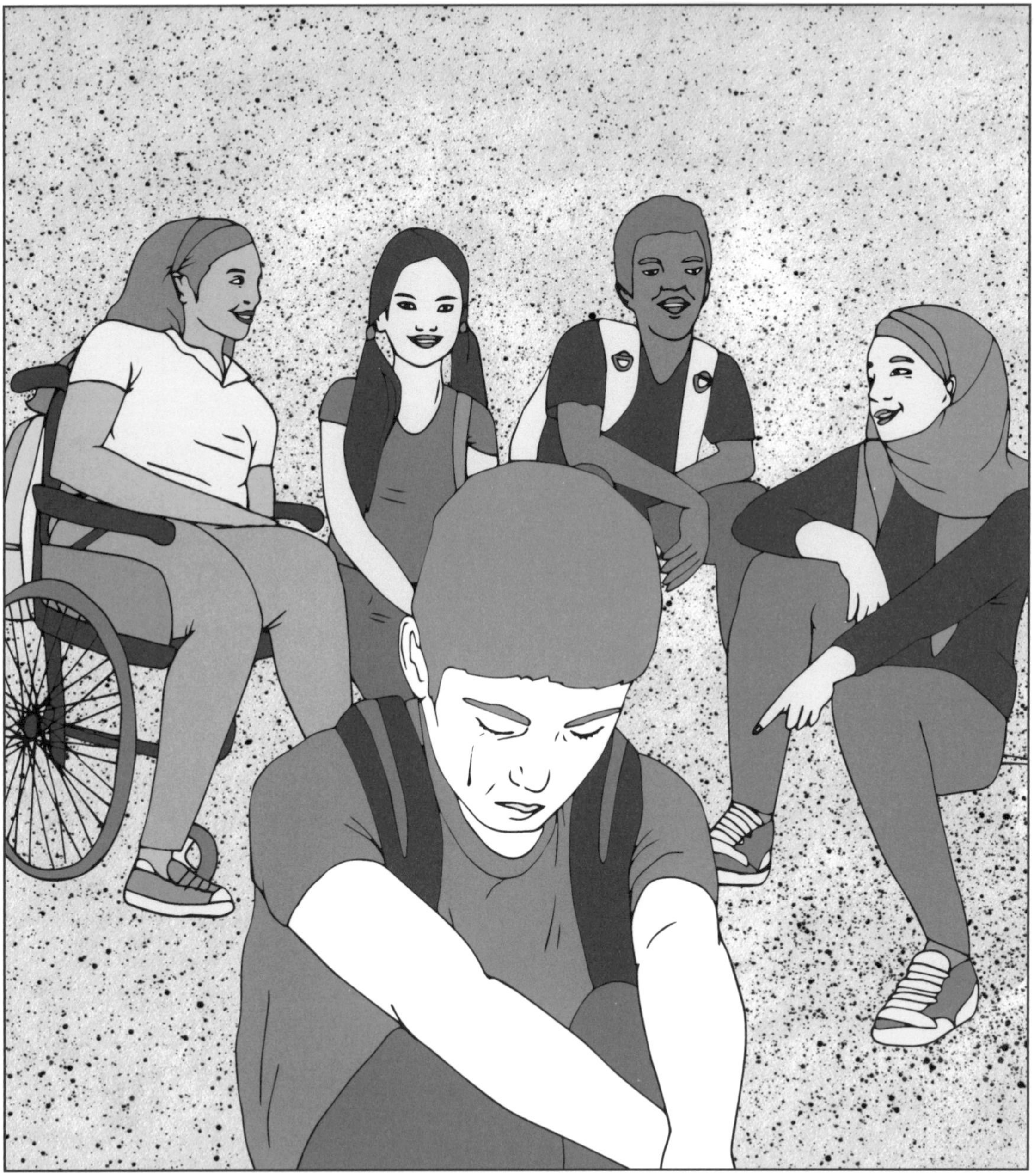

Girls are sick and tired when they hear parents tell their sons, "Don't cry, you're not a girl."

Girls are sick and tired
of hearing that naïveté is
feminine.

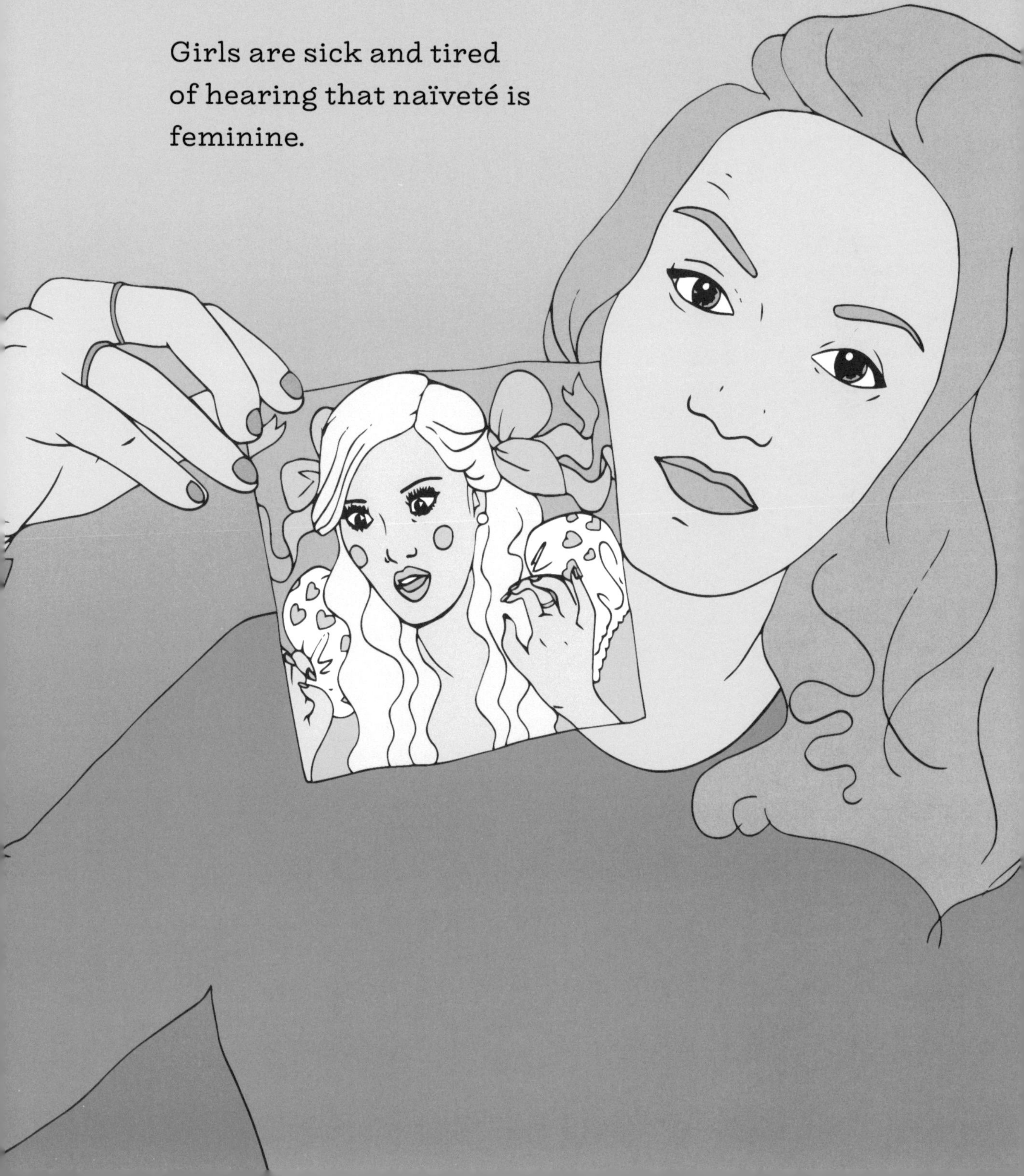

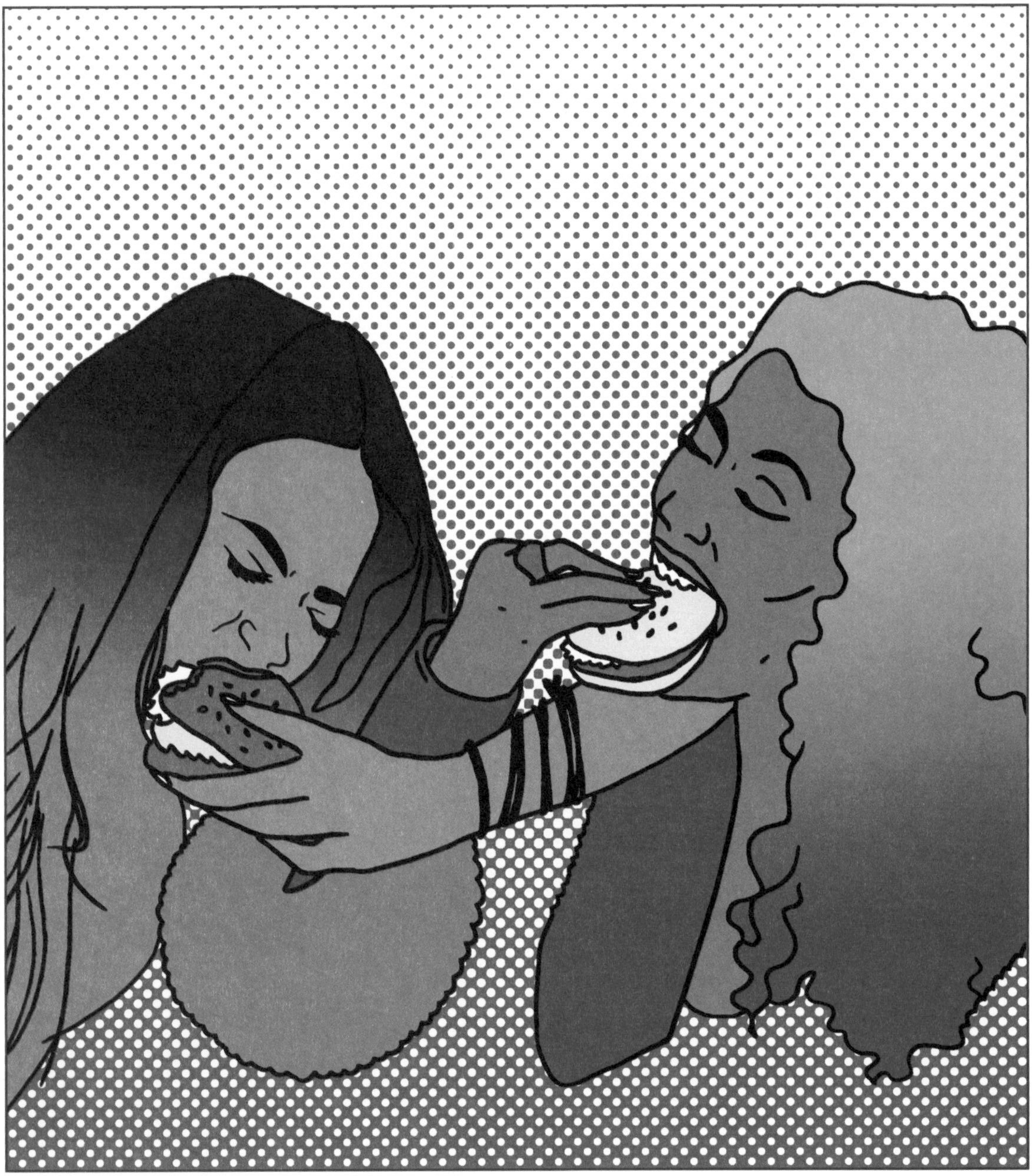

Girls are sick and tired when society criticizes women who drink too much alcohol, who don't want to have children, or who use coarse language.

Girls are sick and tired of cleaning up after their fathers, uncles, brothers, and cousins.

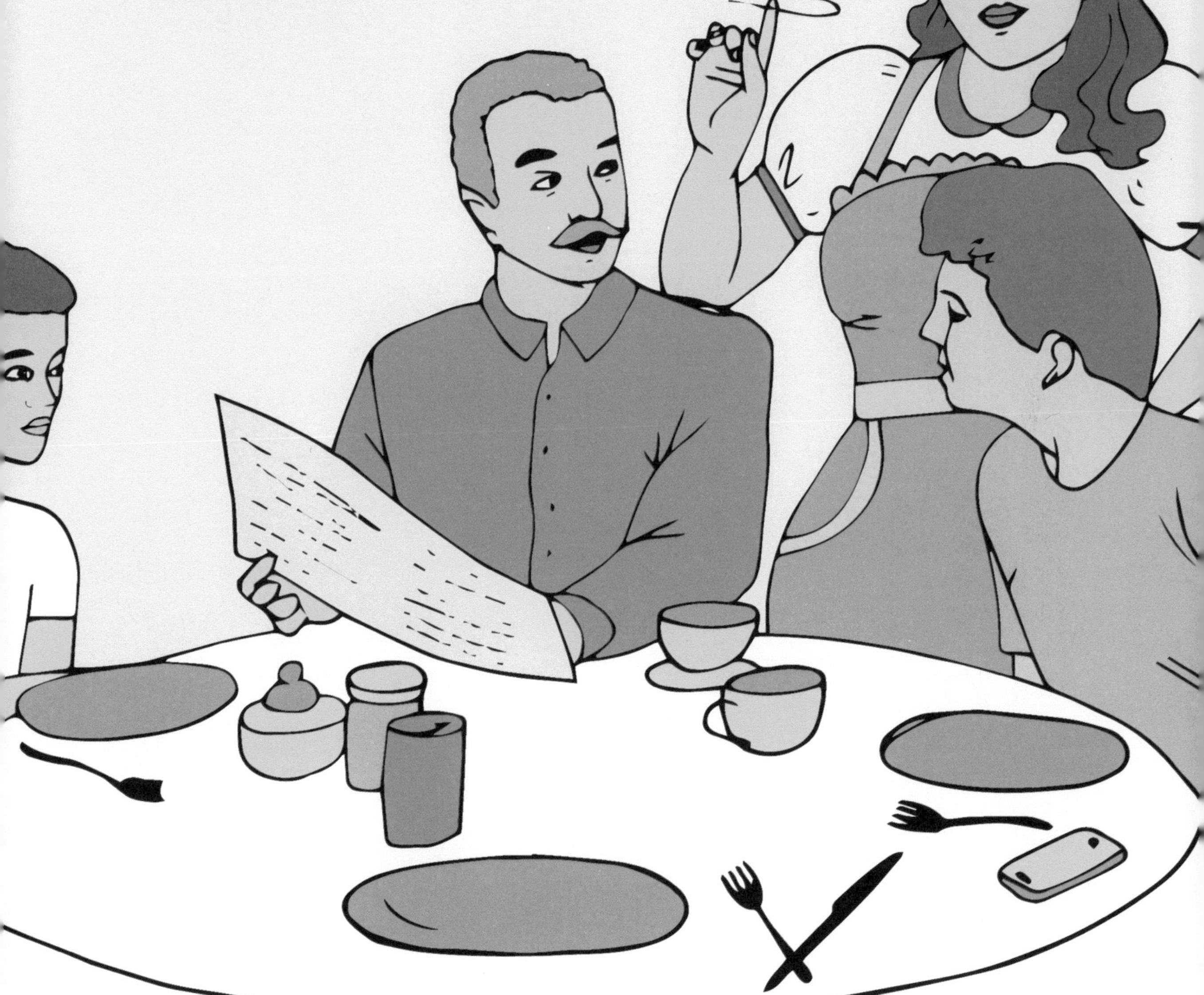

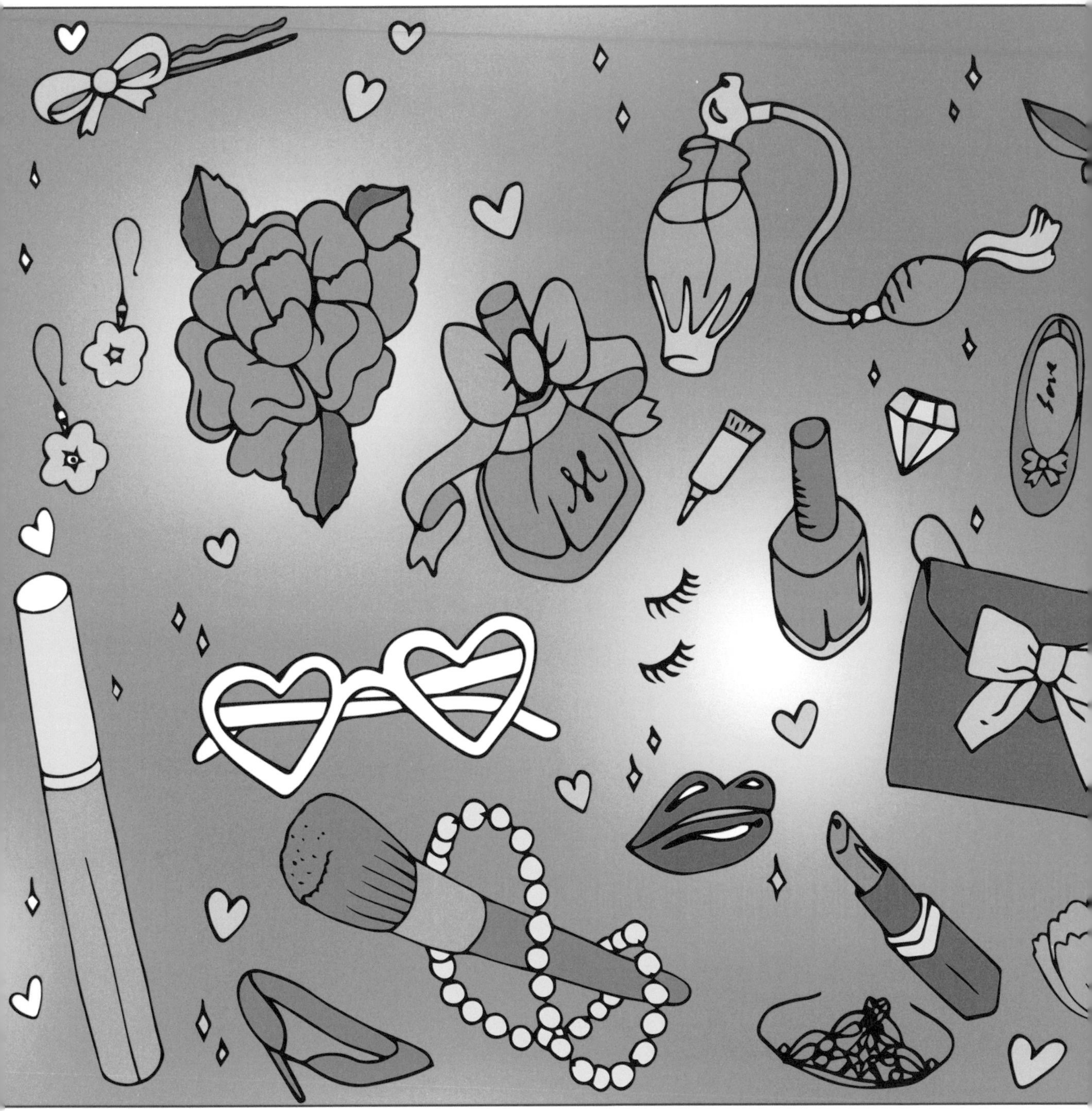
M
love

Girls are sick and tired of people expecting

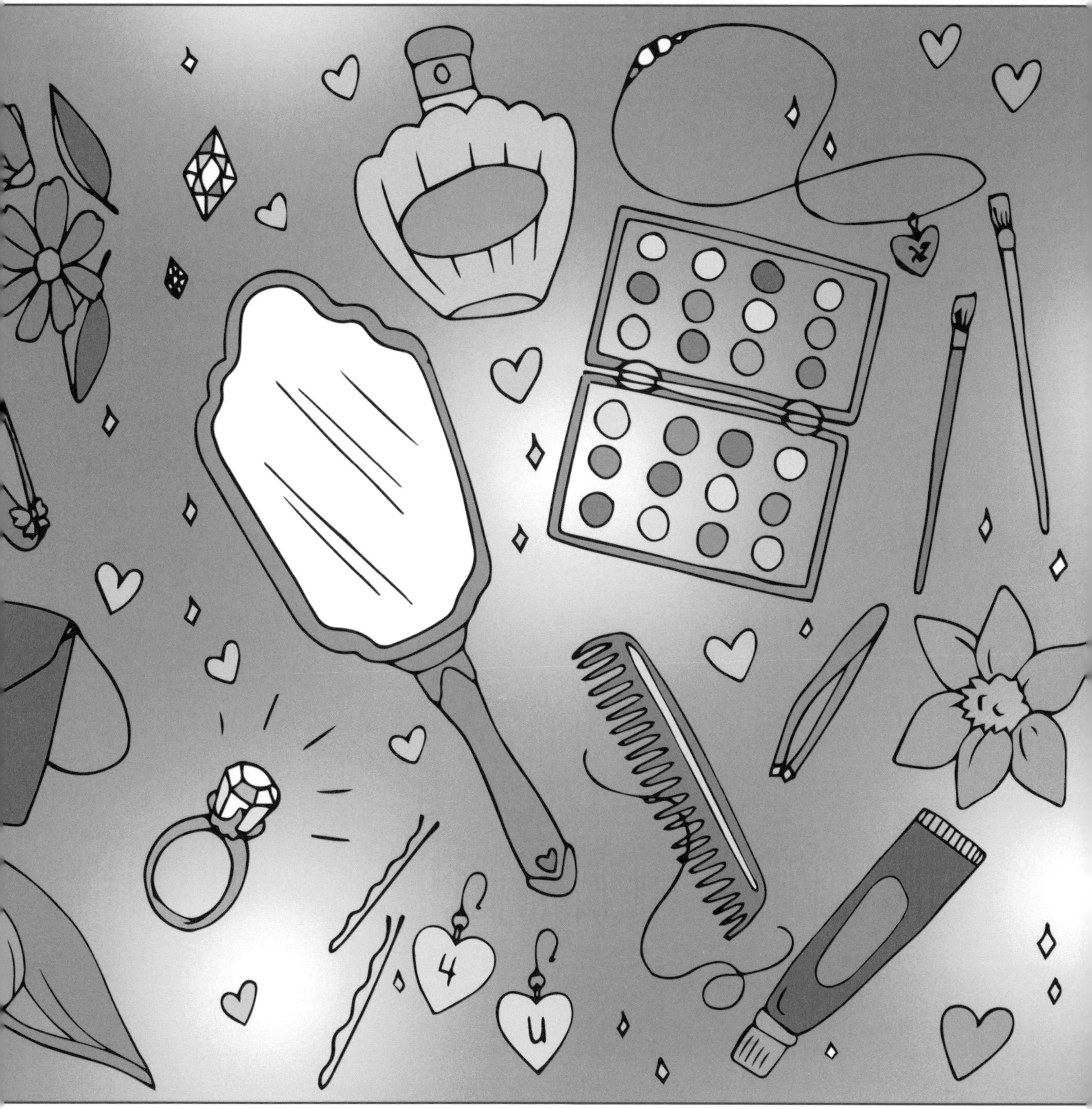
4
U

them to act like princesses from the time they are born.

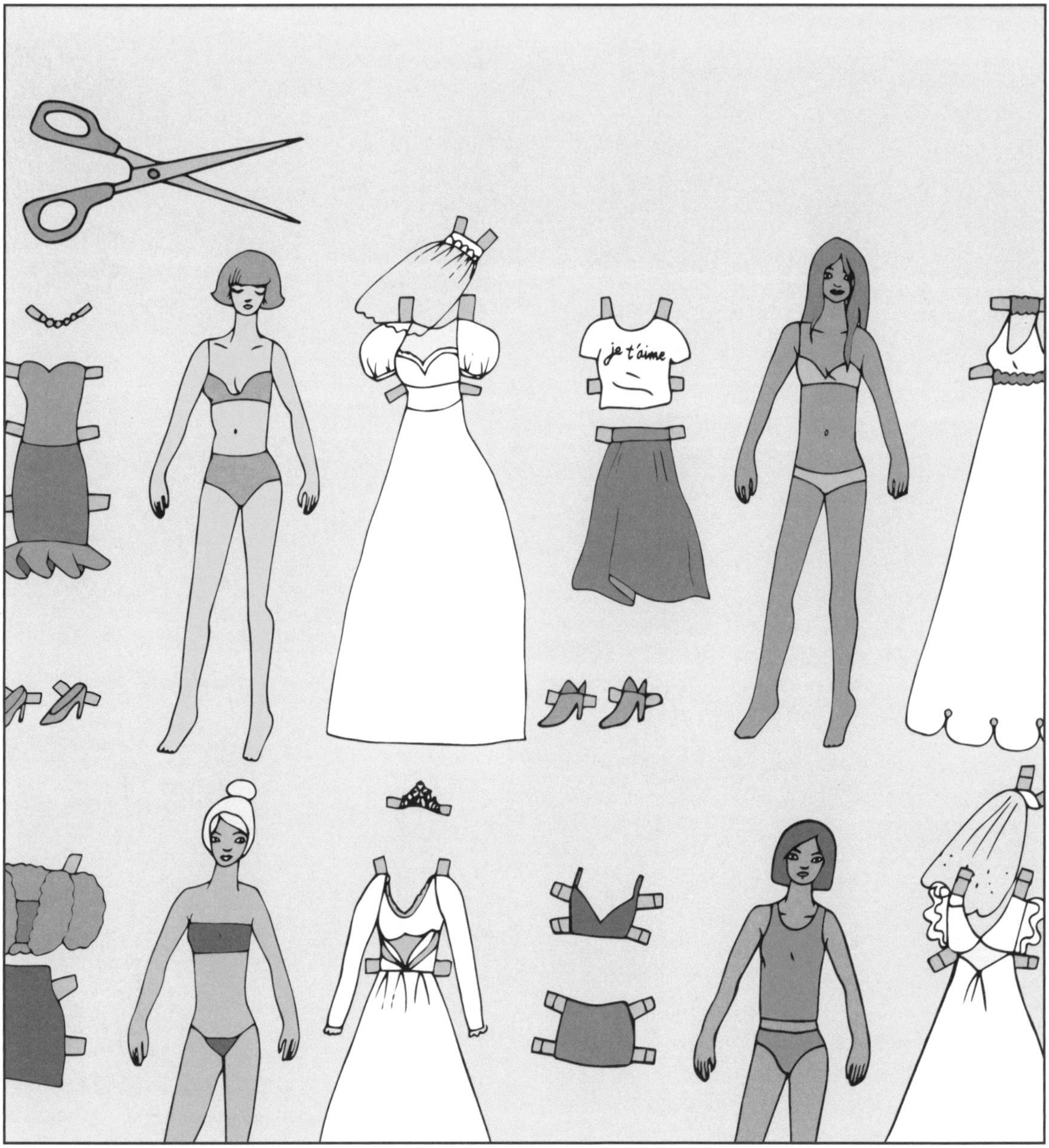
je t'aime

Girls are sick and tired when they think about pre-pubescent girls being forced into marriage to men they've never met. They feel sick to their stomachs for the women who are sold as mail-order brides.

Girls are sick and tired when they hear some guy bragging that he "scored with a chick."

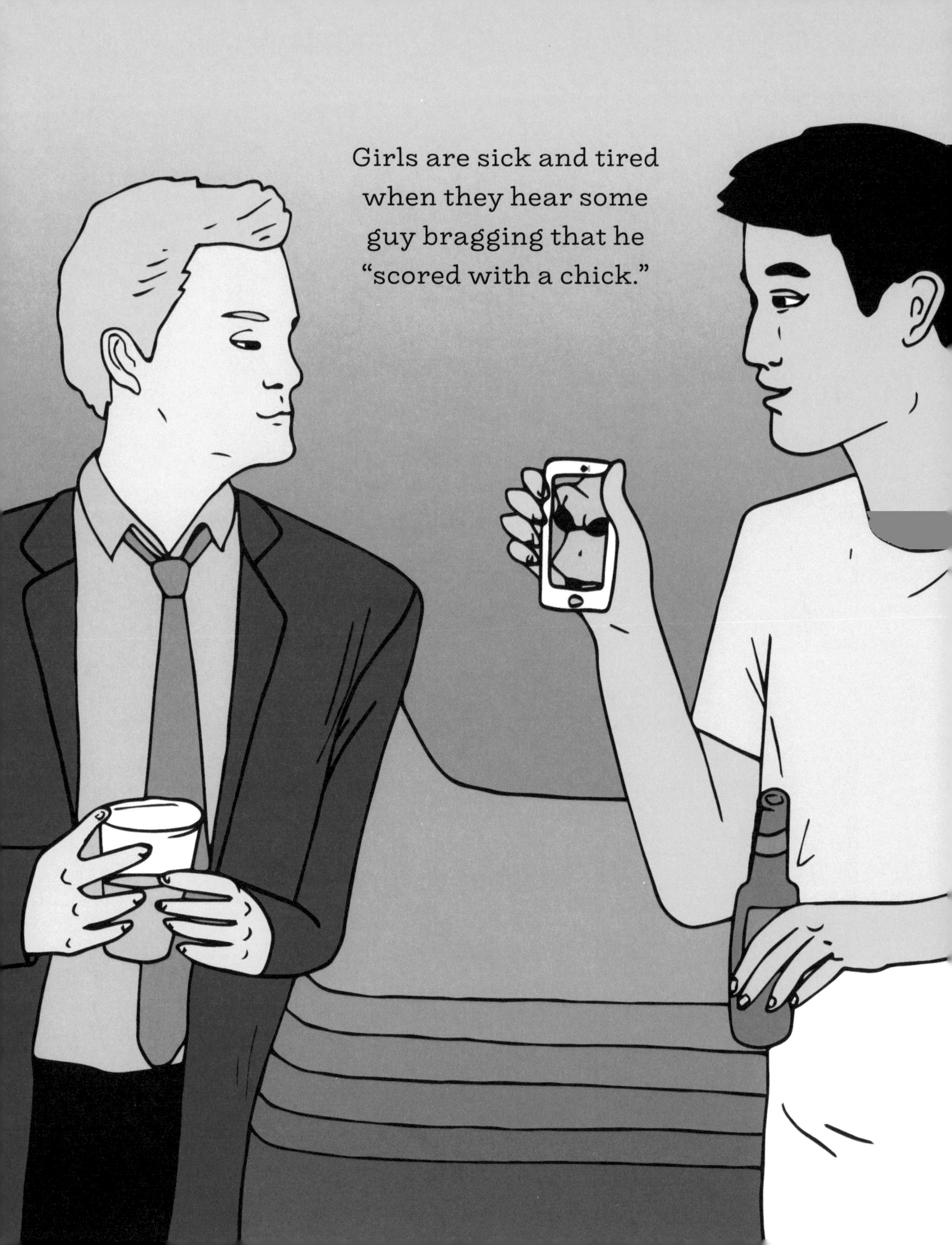

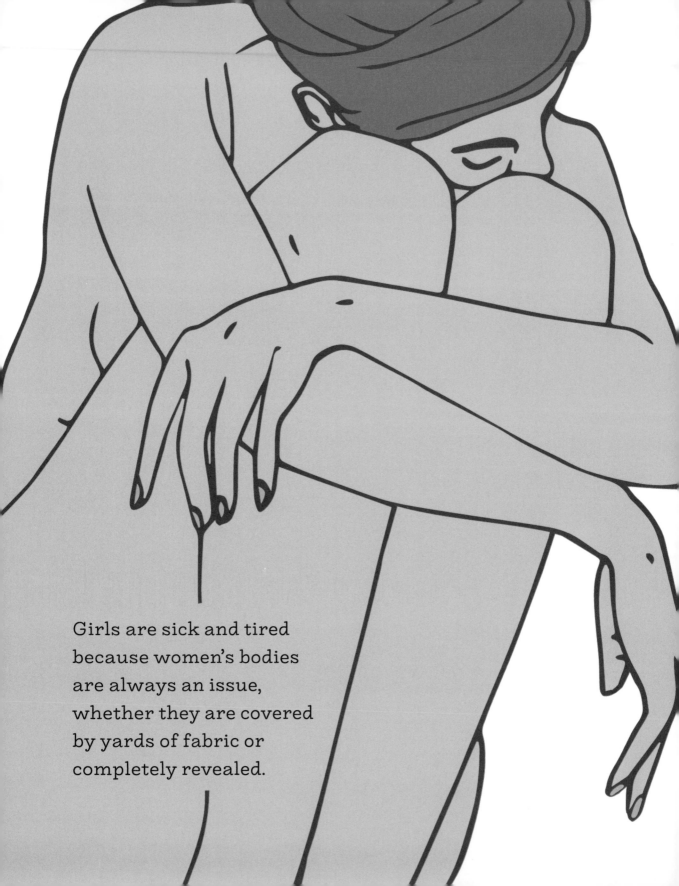

Girls are sick and tired
because women's bodies
are always an issue,
whether they are covered
by yards of fabric or
completely revealed.

Girls are sick and tired of feeling like they have to wear a push-up bra to be sexy, while they have to hide their breasts when nursing a child.

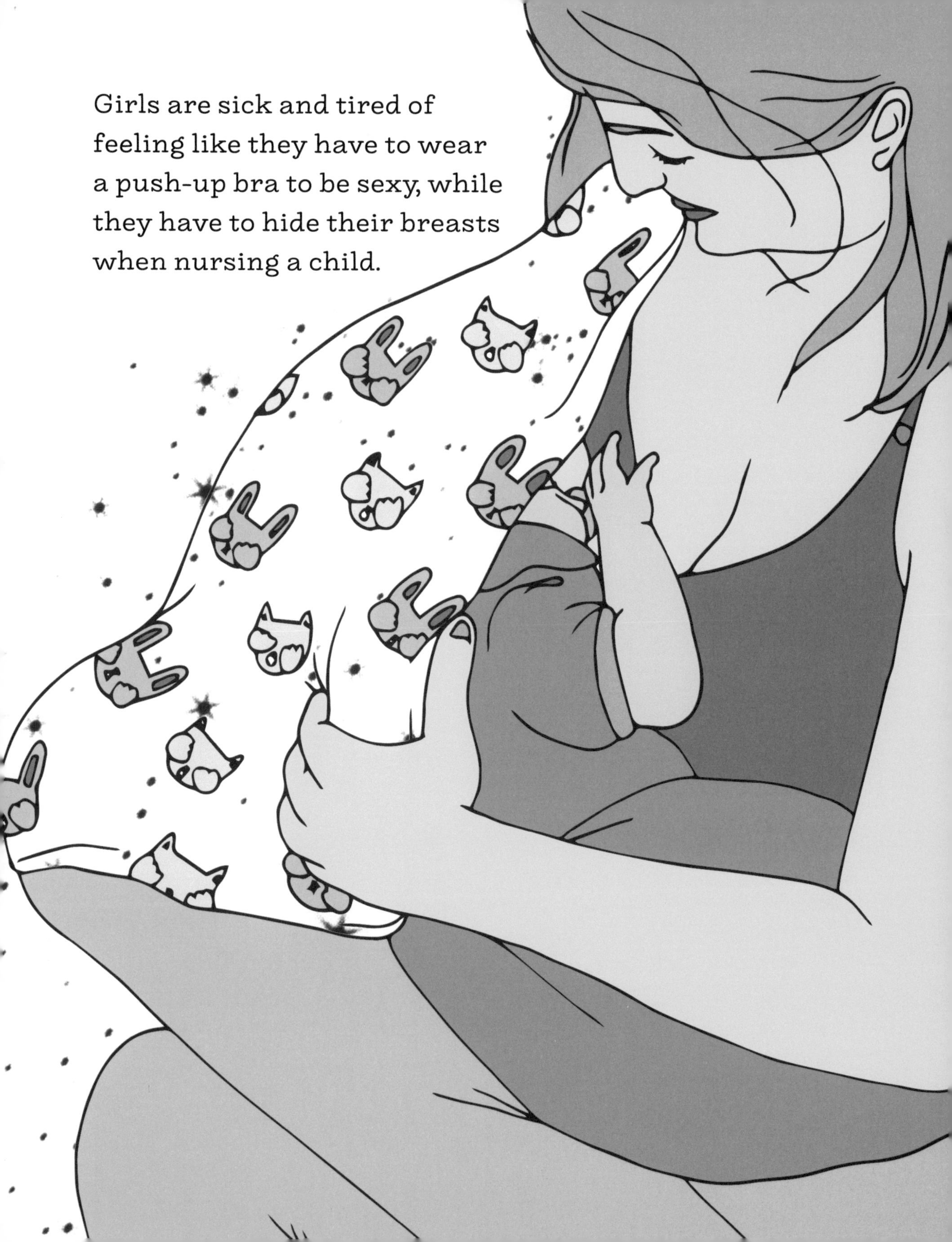

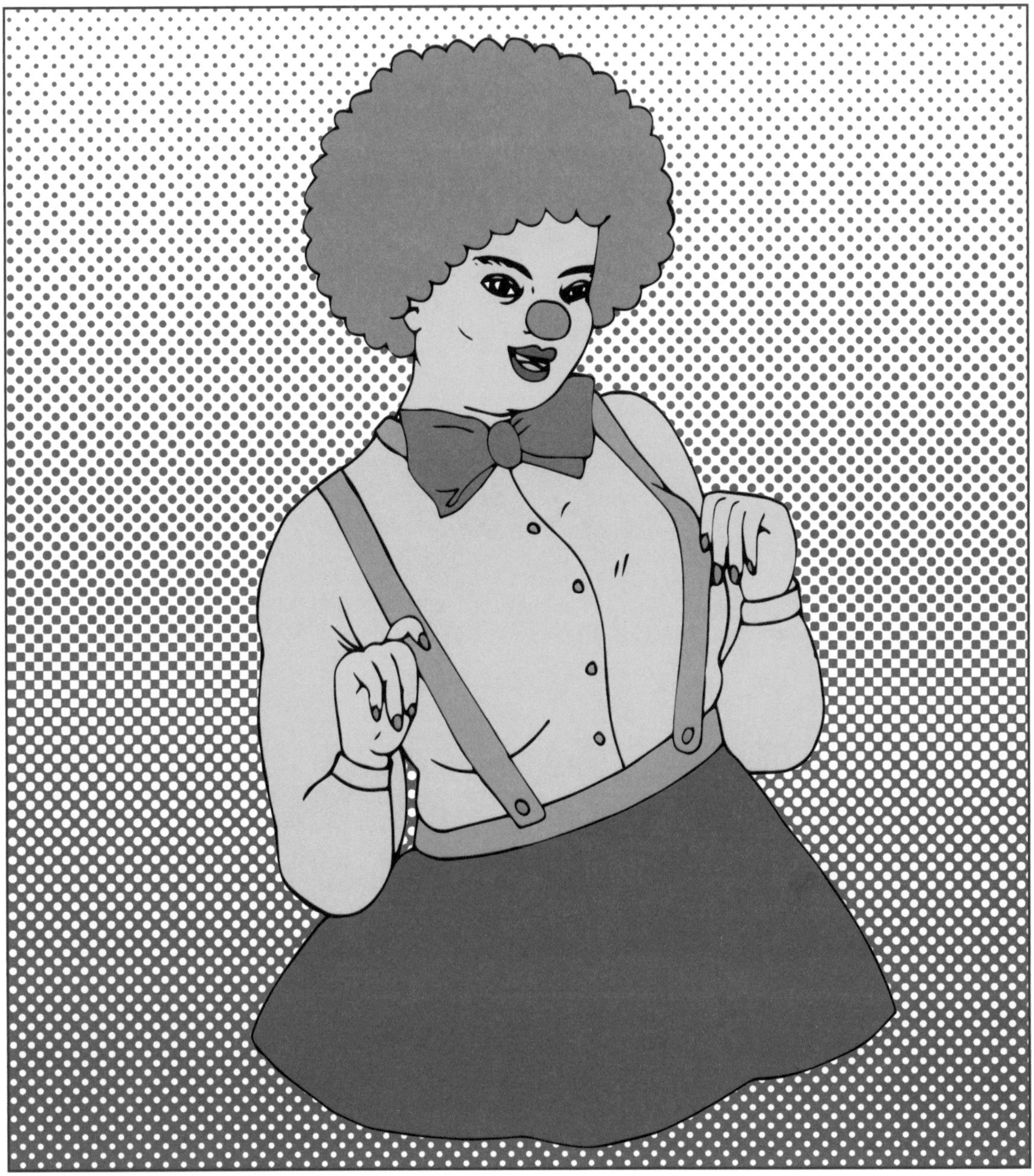

Girls are sick and tired of having to be funny
if they aren't considered "pretty."

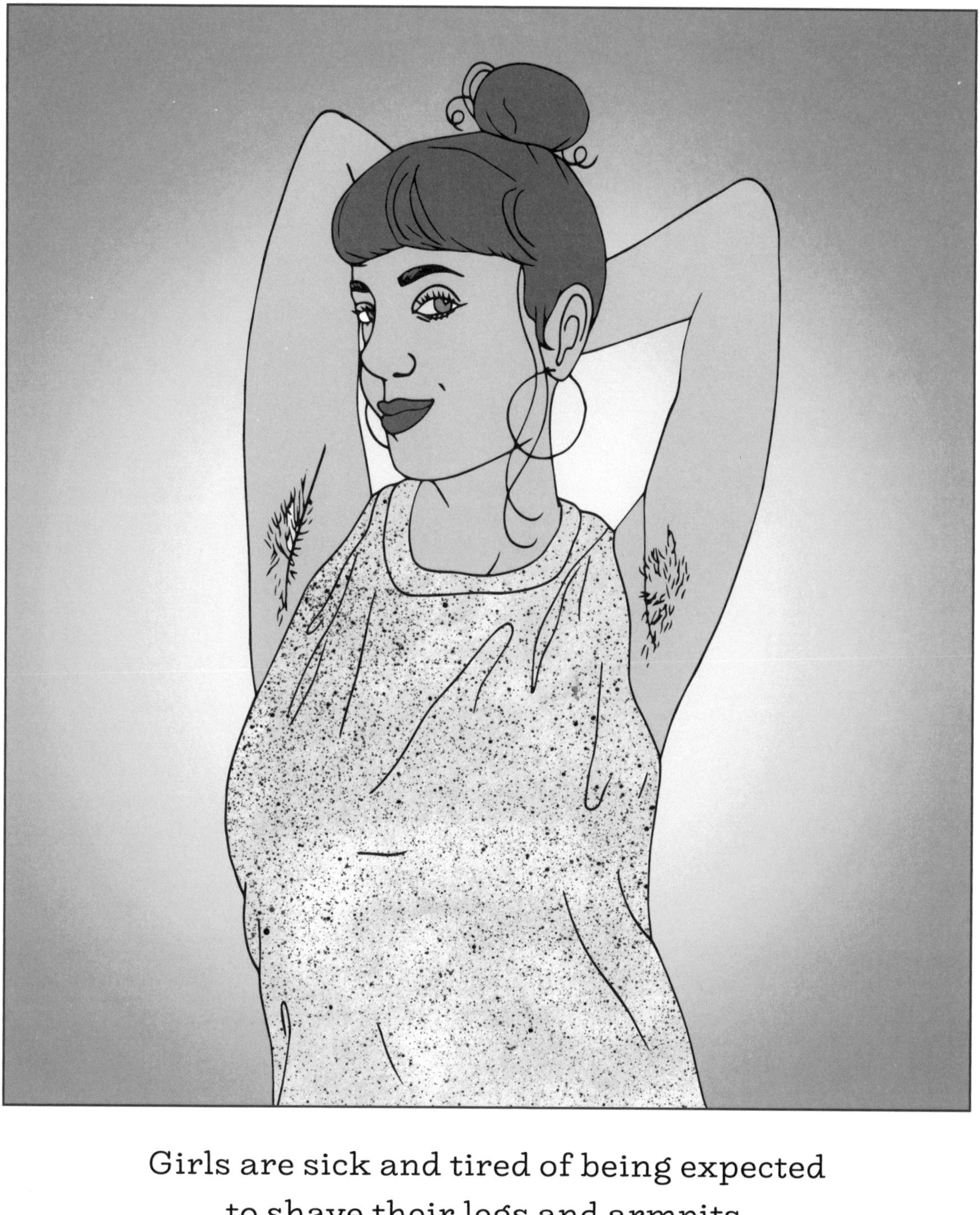

Girls are sick and tired of being expected
to shave their legs and armpits,
and of being judged if they don't.

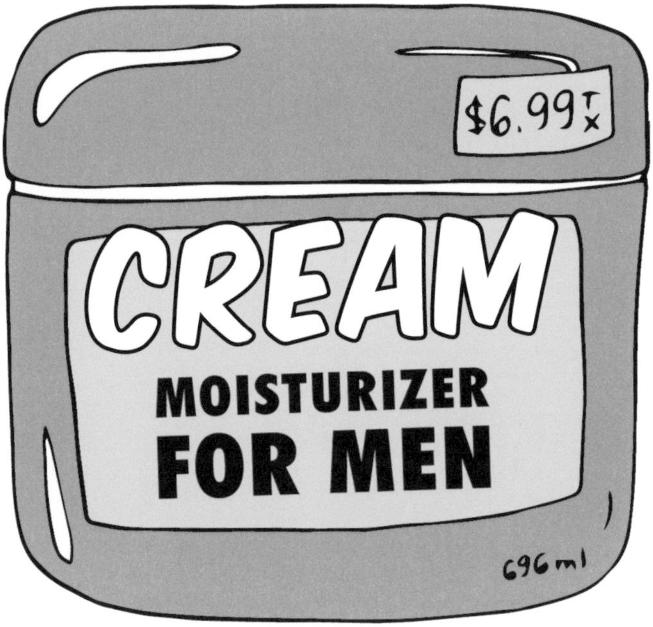
$6.99 TX
CREAM
MOISTURIZER
FOR MEN
696 ml

Girls are sick and tired of paying a "pink tax." Haircuts, cosmetic creams, deodorant, shoes, jeans, and razors—all of them cost more for women than for men.

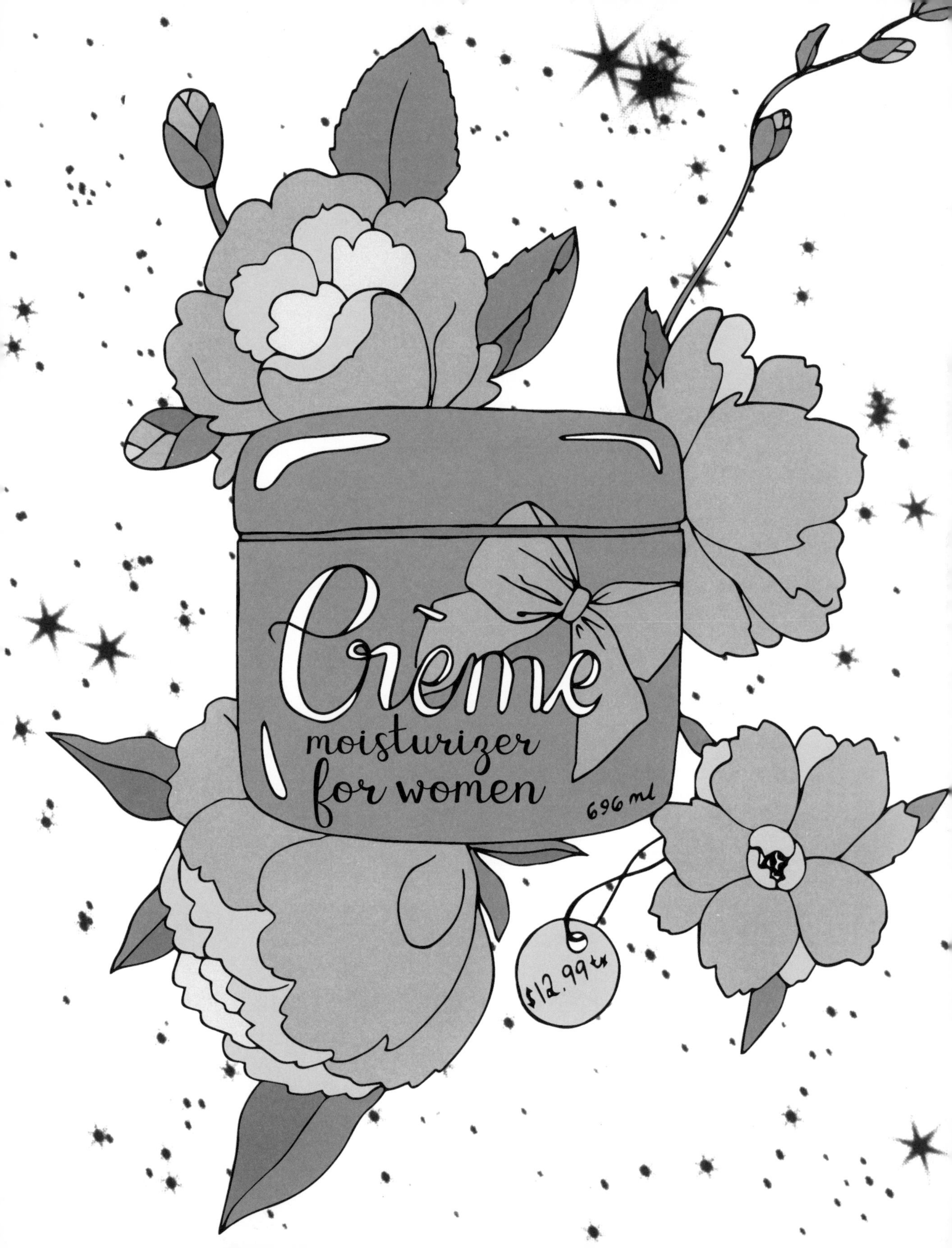
Crème
moisturizer
for women
696 ml
$12.99+tx

Girls are sick and tired of constantly finding fault with themselves for never looking like the digitally altered girls in magazines.

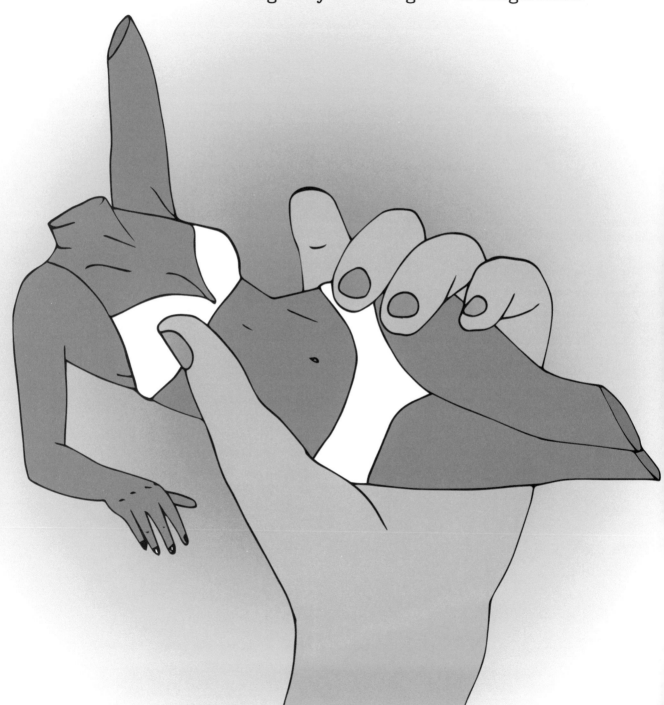

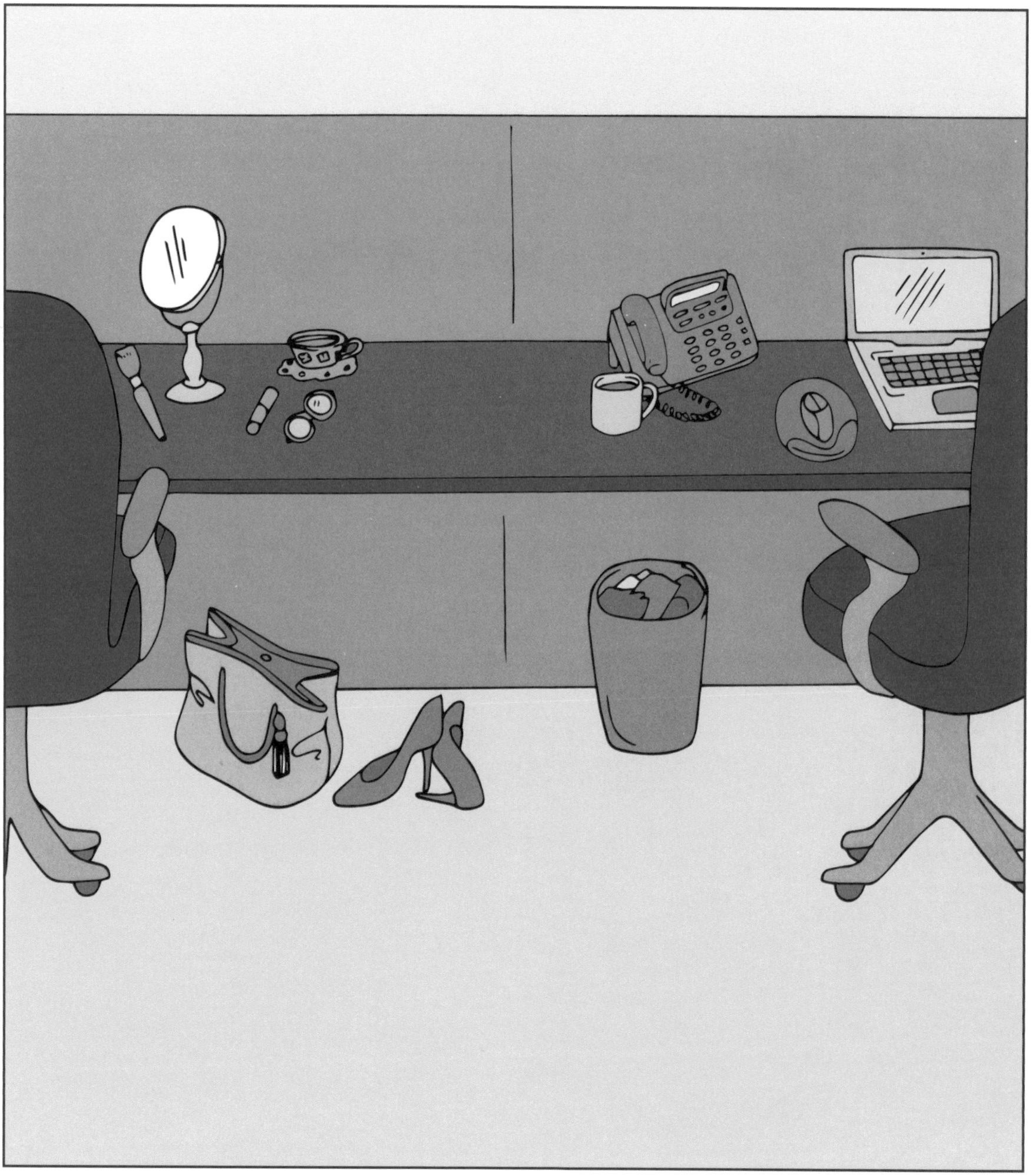

Girls are sick and tired of being told that they were hired for their looks and complimented on their appearance before their intelligence.

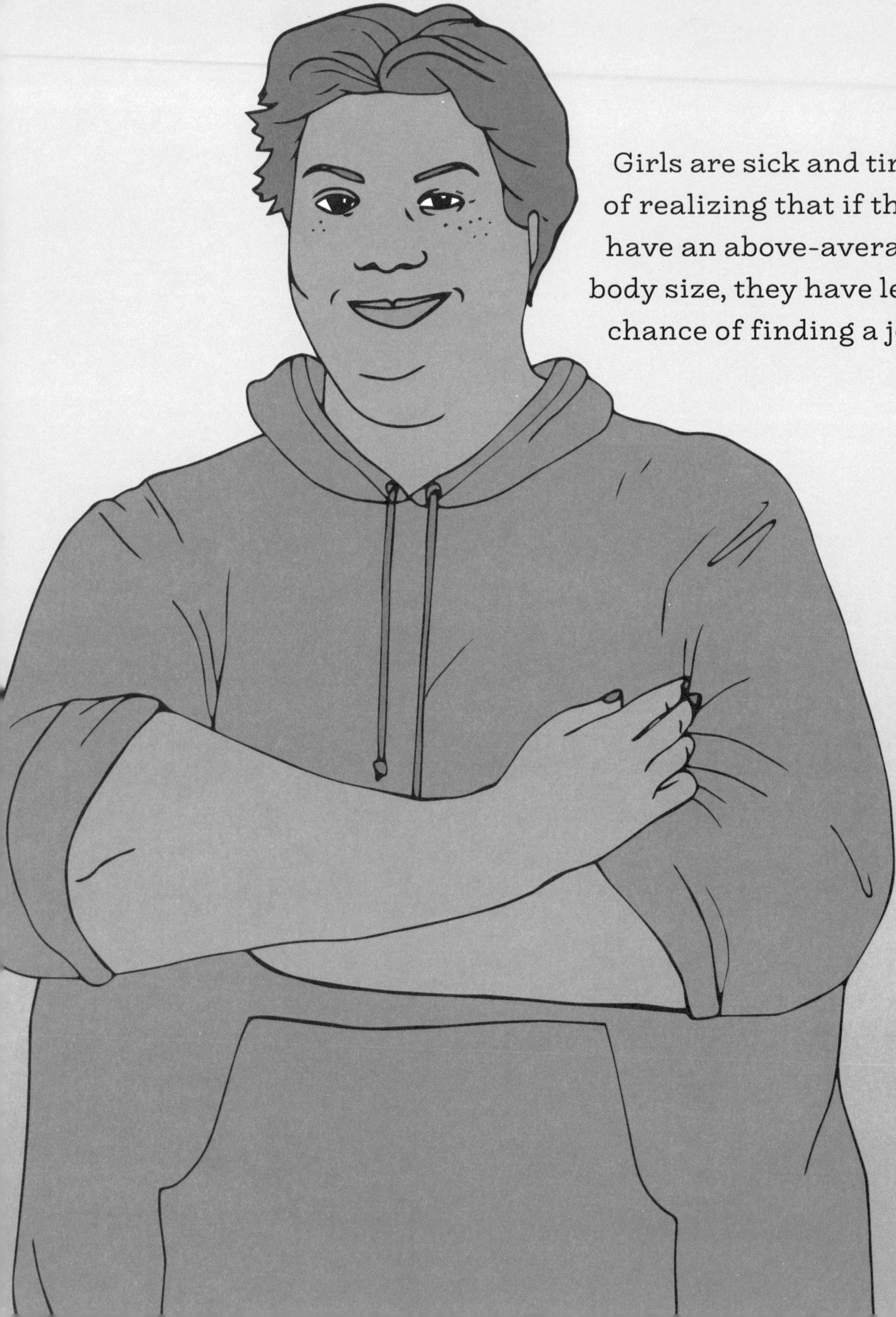

Girls are sick and tired of realizing that if they have an above-average body size, they have less chance of finding a job.

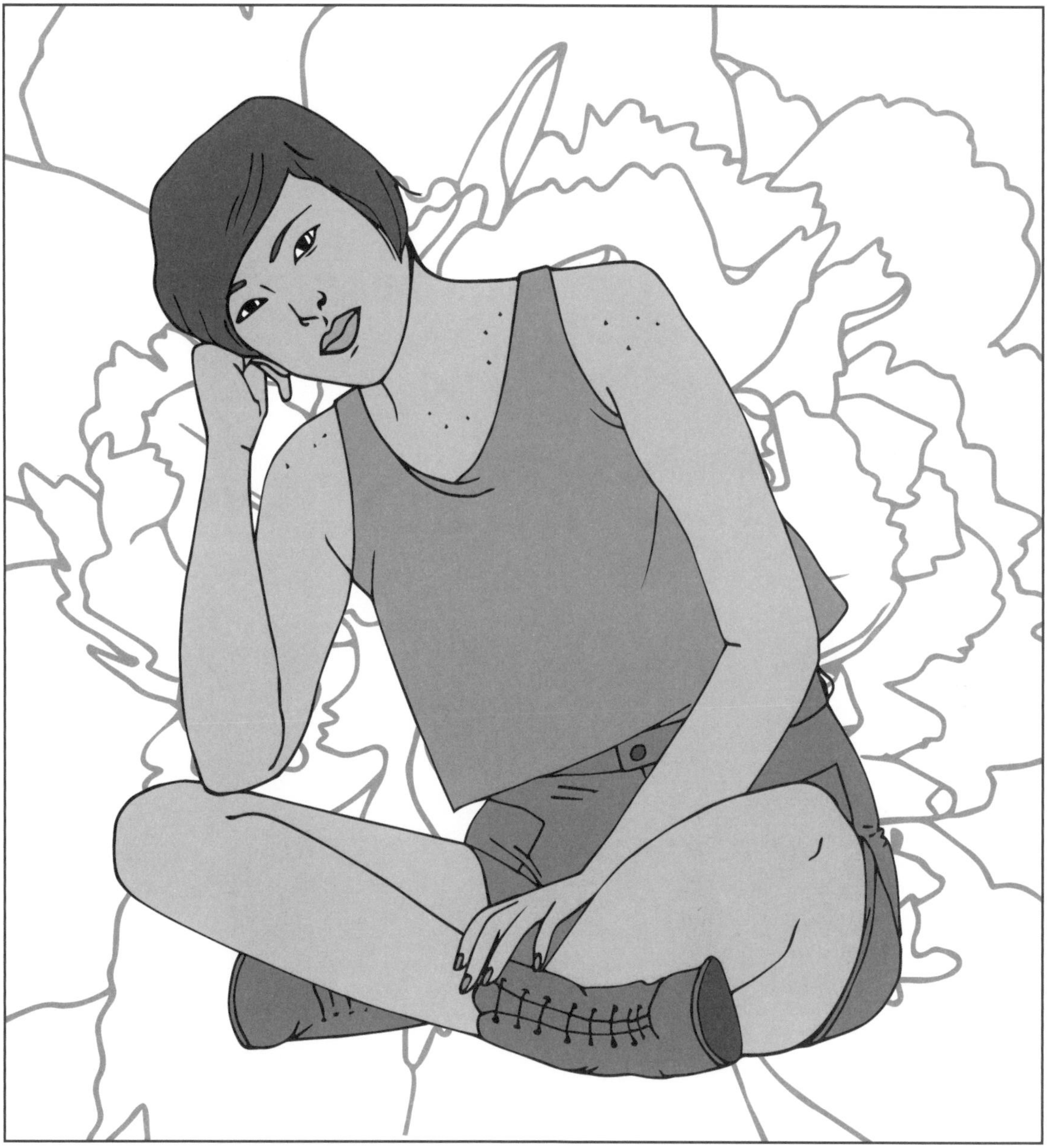

Girls are sick and tired when trans and gender-diverse people do not have the gender they identify with recognized in day-to-day life, by the media, by institutions...

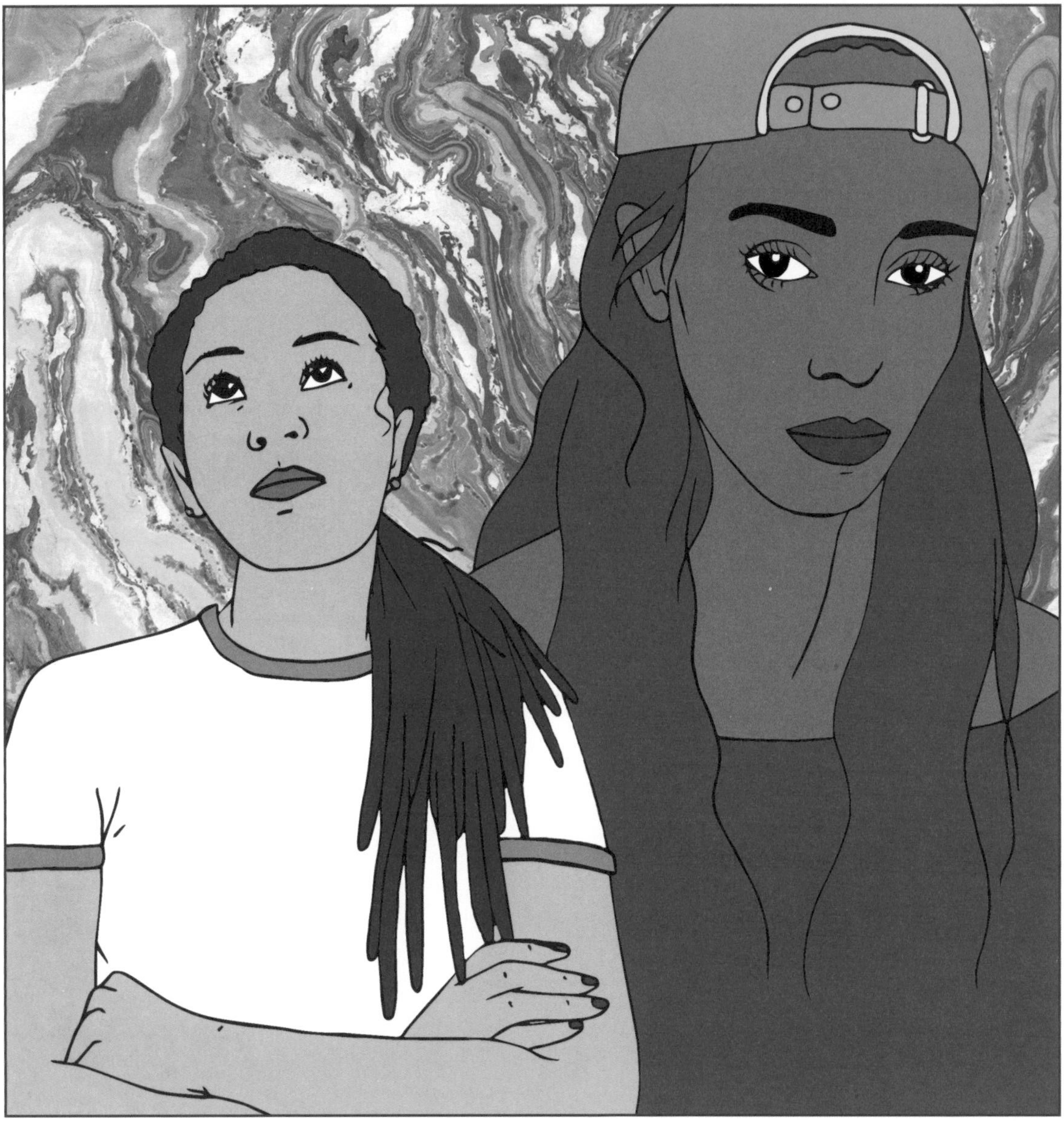

Racialized girls are sick and tired of being asked where they're "really" from and being doubted if they say "I was born here." They are sick and tired of being stereotyped and underrepresented in media, film, public events, and politics.

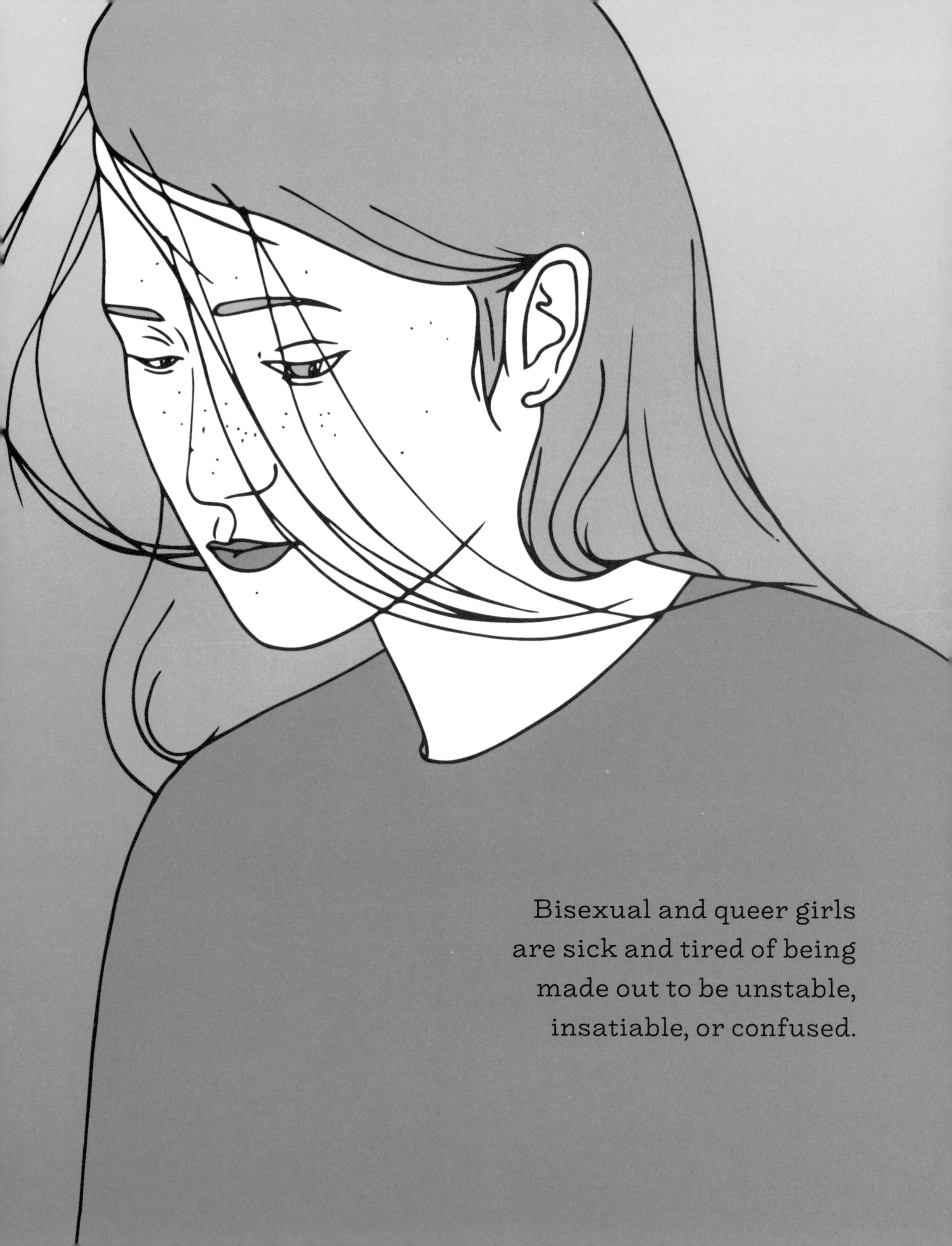

Bisexual and queer girls
are sick and tired of being
made out to be unstable,
insatiable, or confused.

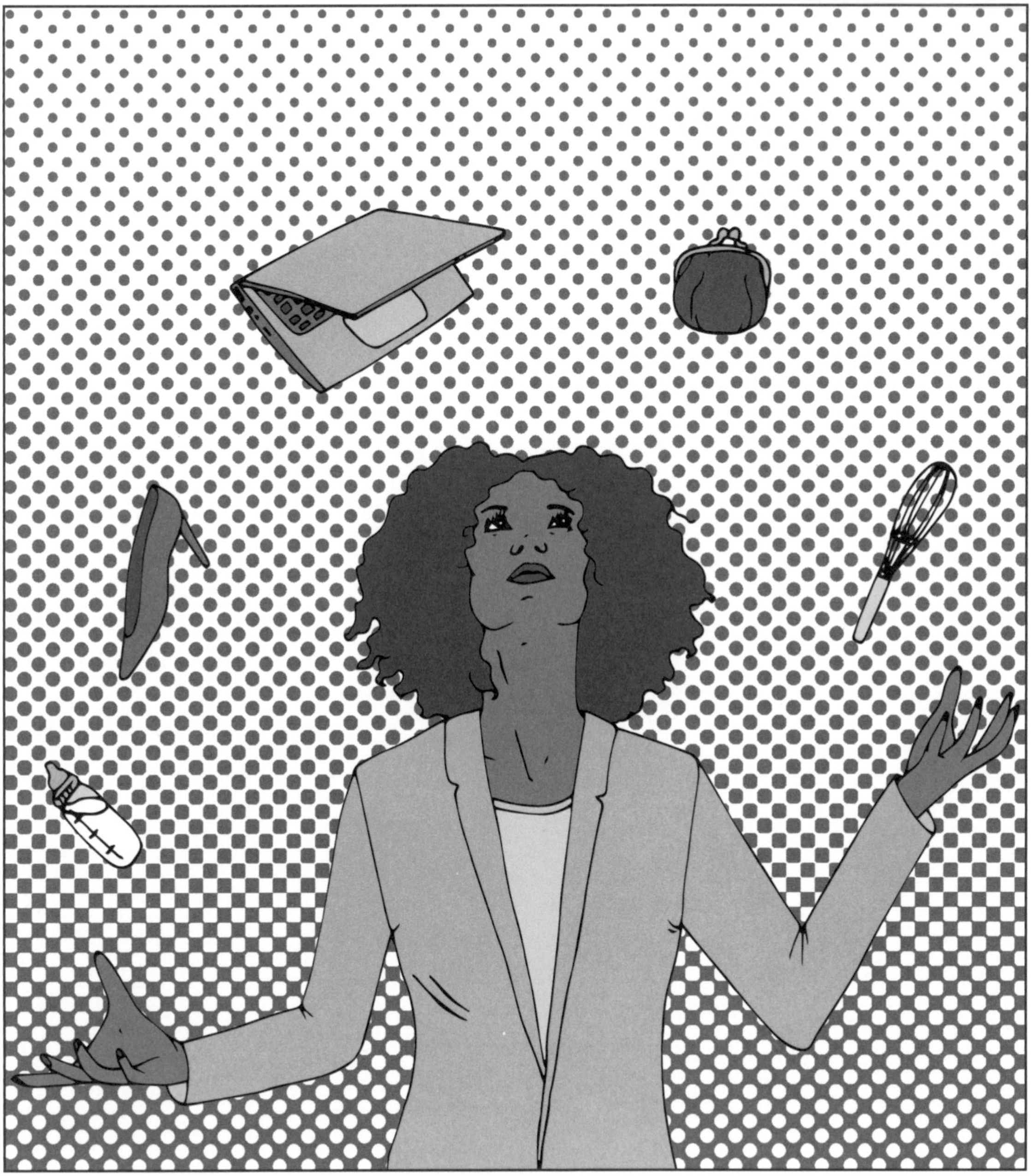

Girls are sick and tired when men who cook and do the shopping are praised for being modern, while for women it's just considered normal.

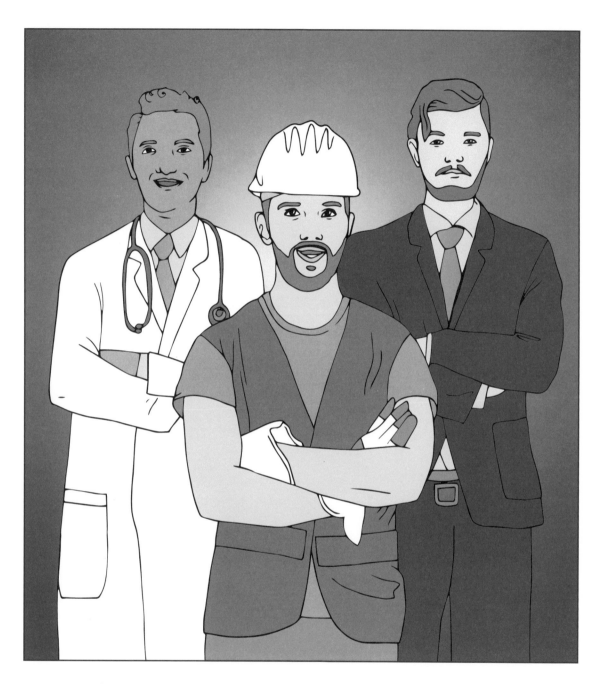

Girls are sick and tired that they have to change
the titles of certain jobs because it was never
imagined that a woman could do them.

Girls are sick and tired of knowing that on average, worldwide, women earn 32% less than men for the same work, and that recent statistics show that it will take another 100 years to close that gap.*

* World Economic Forum Global Gender Gap Report 2017: Key Findings

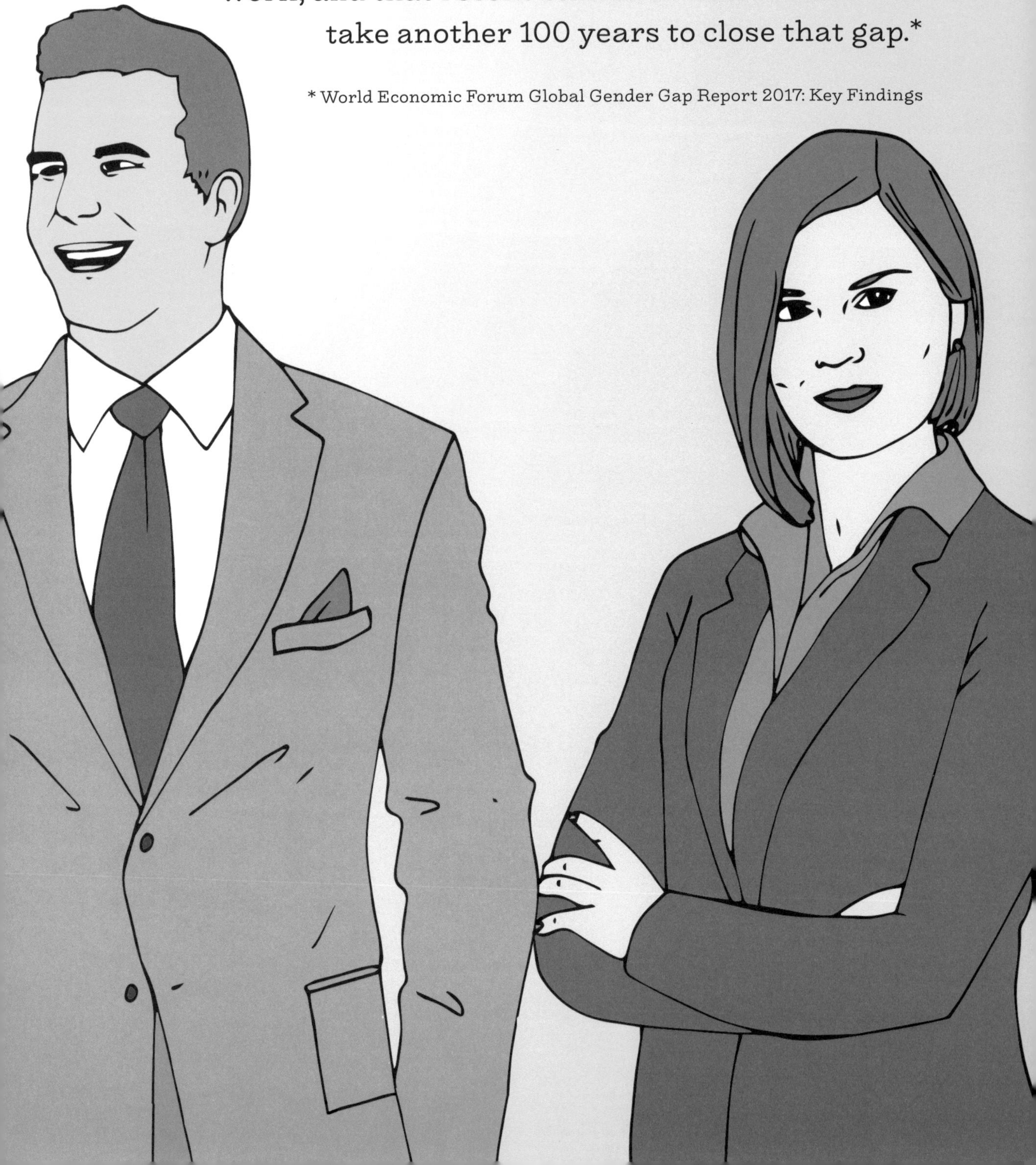

Girls are sick and tired of knowing that in Canada, for equal work, Indigenous, racialized, and immigrant women, as well as women with disabilities, all earn on average less than white women.*

* Canadianwomen.org/thefacts: The Wage Gap

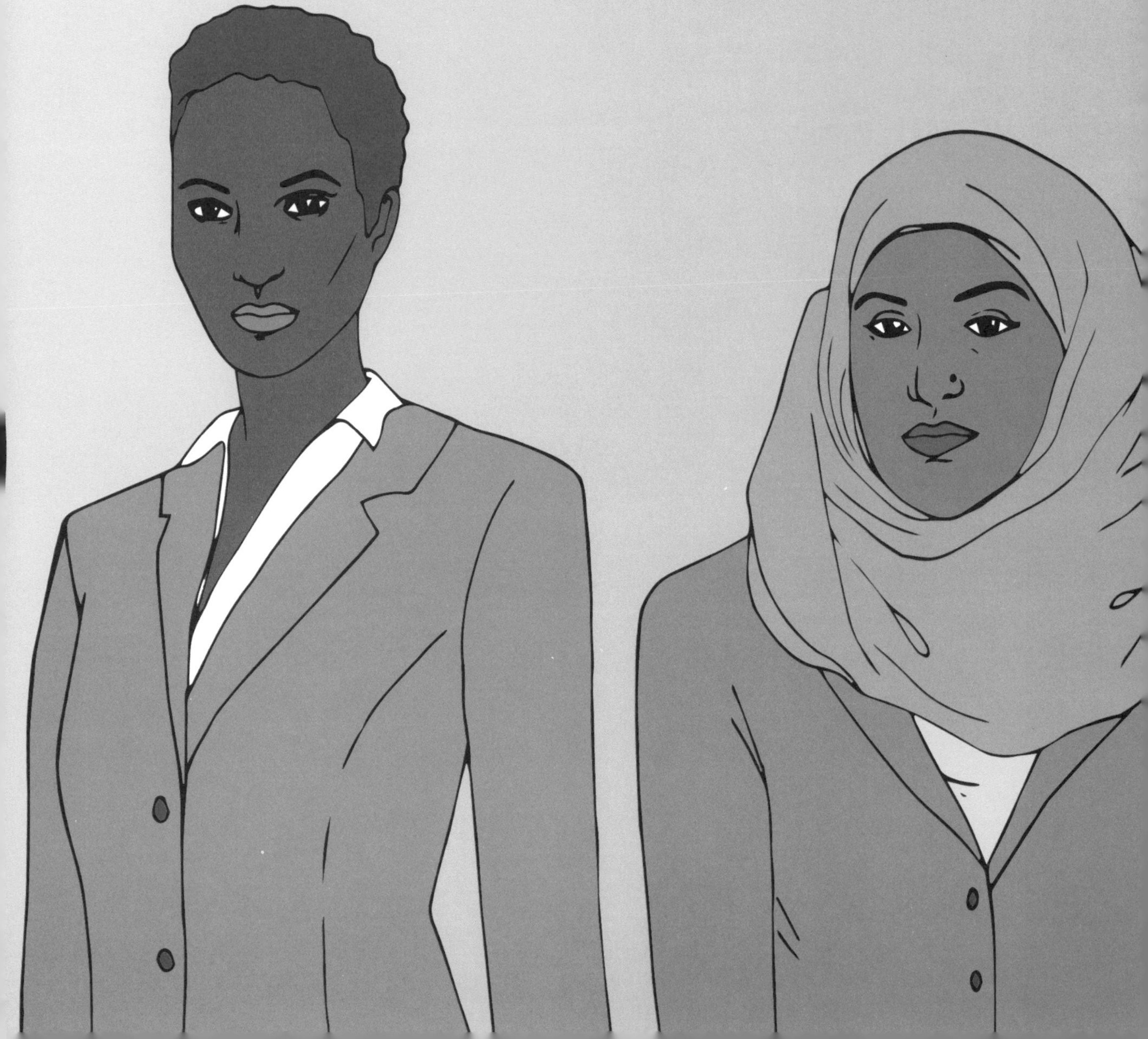

Girls are sick and tired
of being stoned, kidnapped,
exiled, and subjected to
genital mutilation in the
name of cultural tradition.

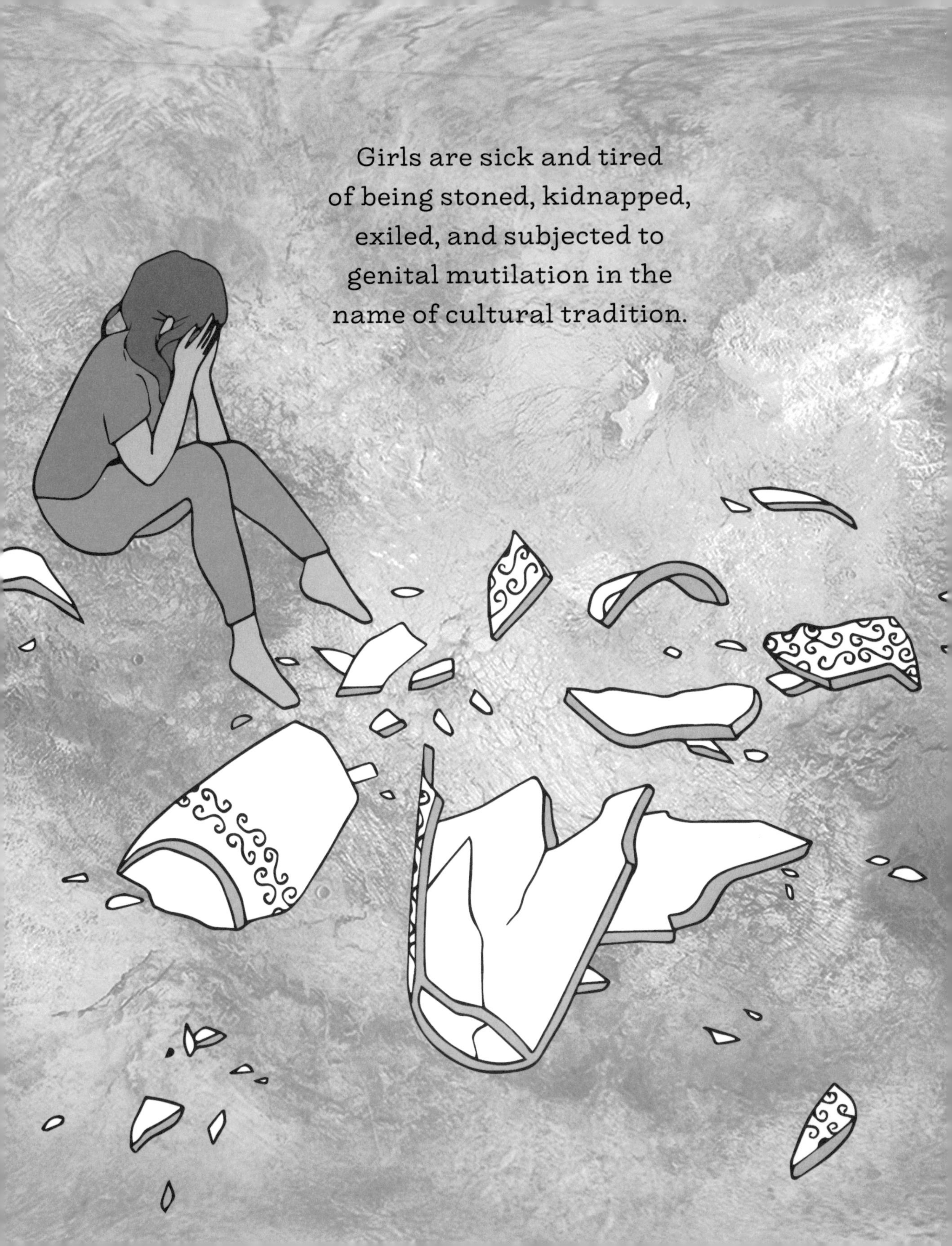

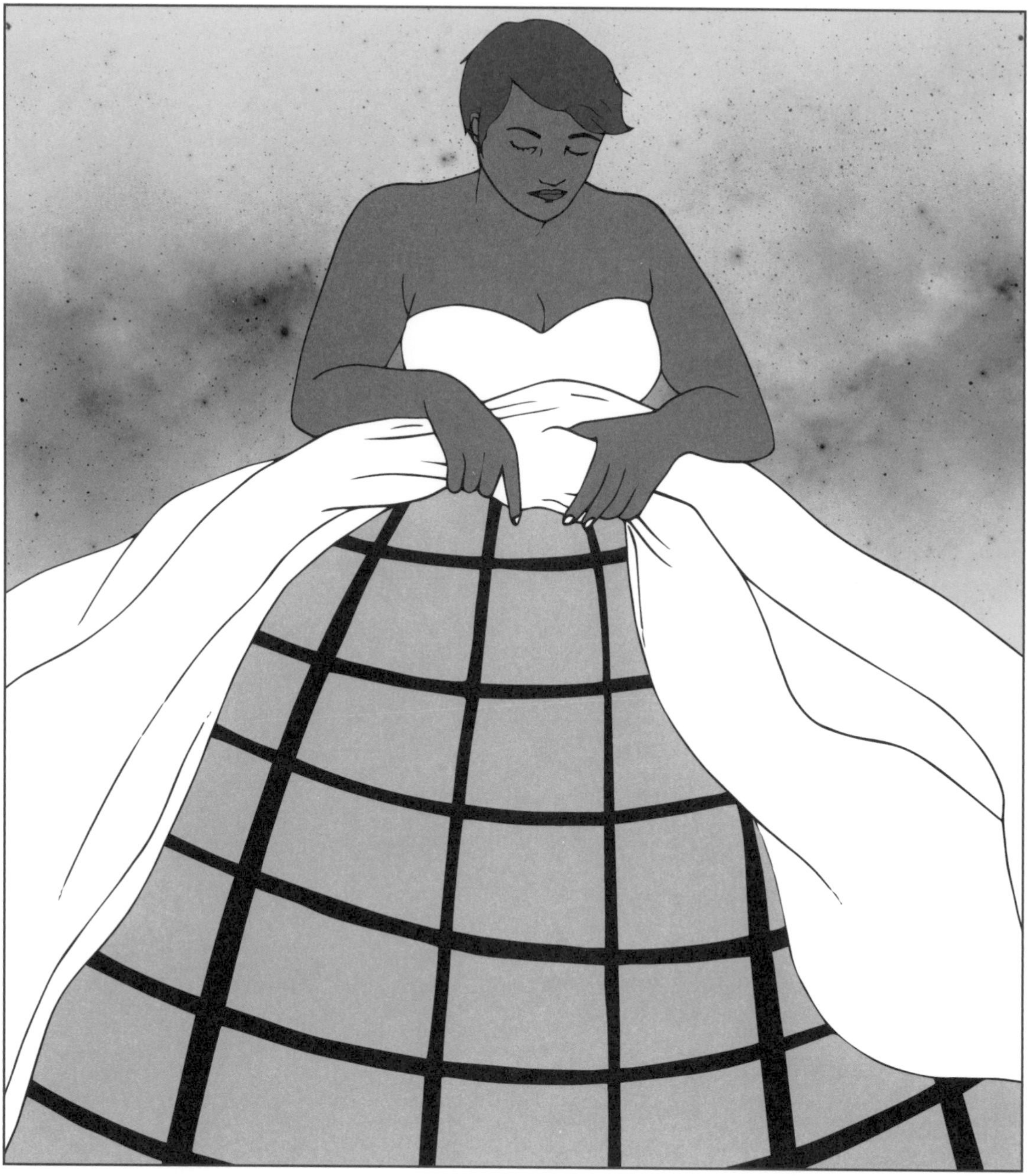

Girls are sick and tired of contraception and abortion being women's issues, and that society can prevent them from having both.

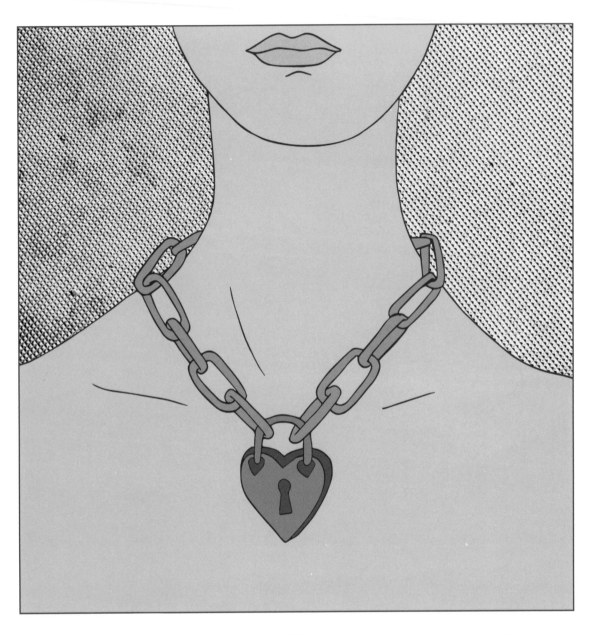

Girls are sick and tired of knowing that even today
women are the victims of honor crimes and are treated
as "sub-human." They are sick and tired that in many
countries, rape is not considered a crime and women
are not in control of their own bodies.

Girls are sick and tired of being used as prizes in armed conflicts; of being raped when their cities and houses are pillaged in the chaos of war.

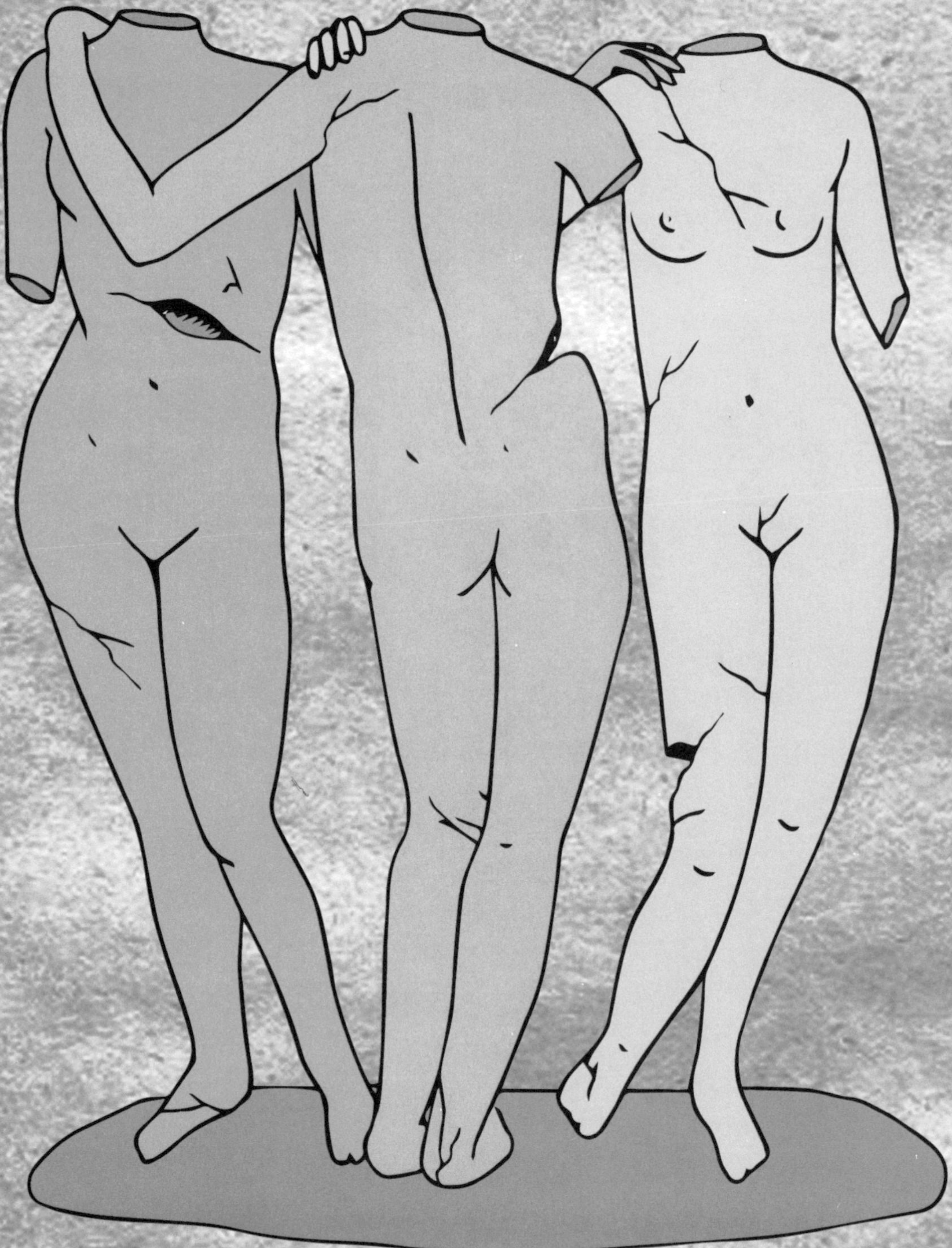

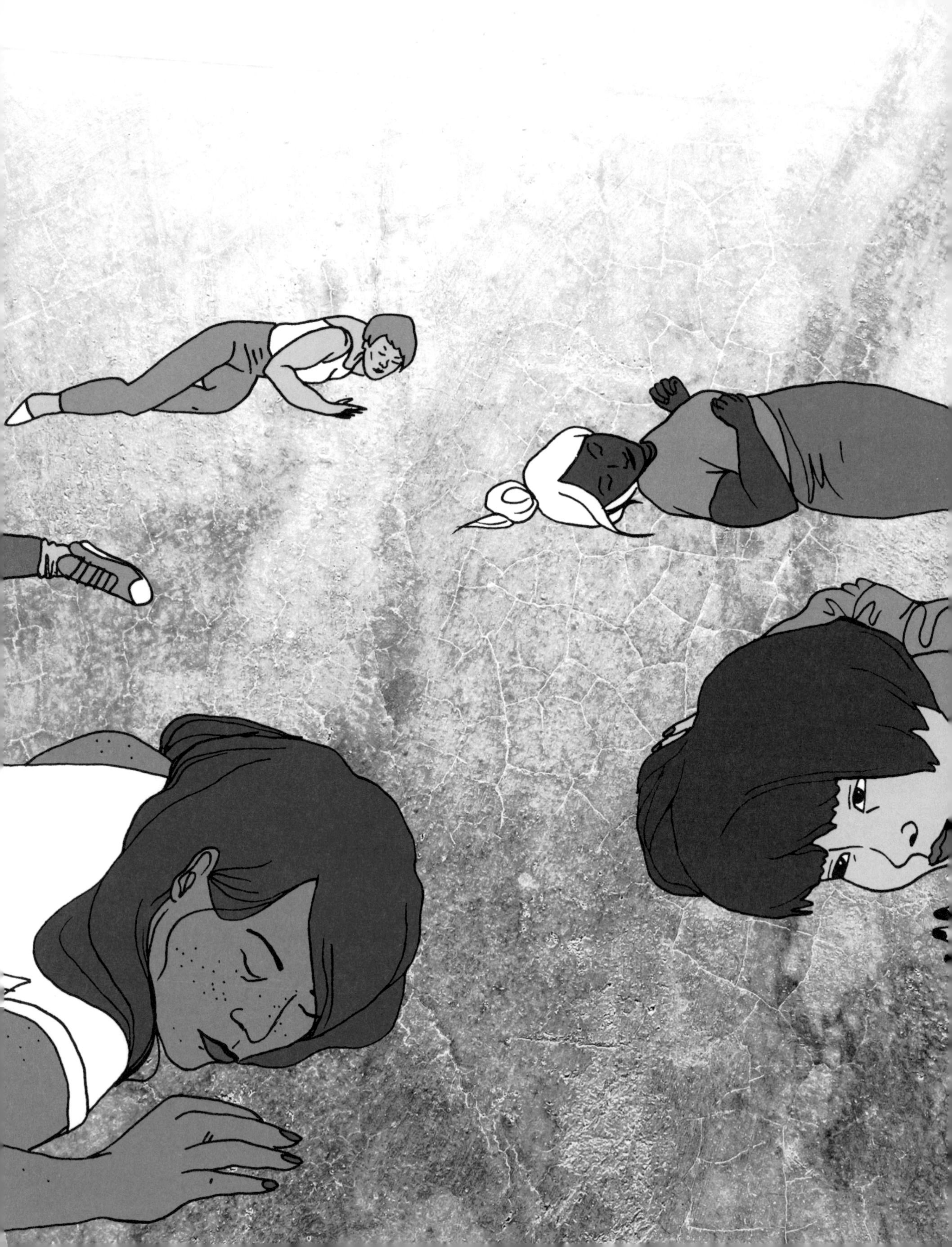

Girls are sick and tired of knowing that
globally women between the ages of 15 and 44
are more likely to die of rape and violence than
cancer, car accidents, war, and malaria combined.*

* United Nations UNiTE Campaign 2015

Indigenous girls are sick and tired because, in North America, they are five times more likely to die of violence than other women their age.*

* United Nations UNiTE Campaign 2015

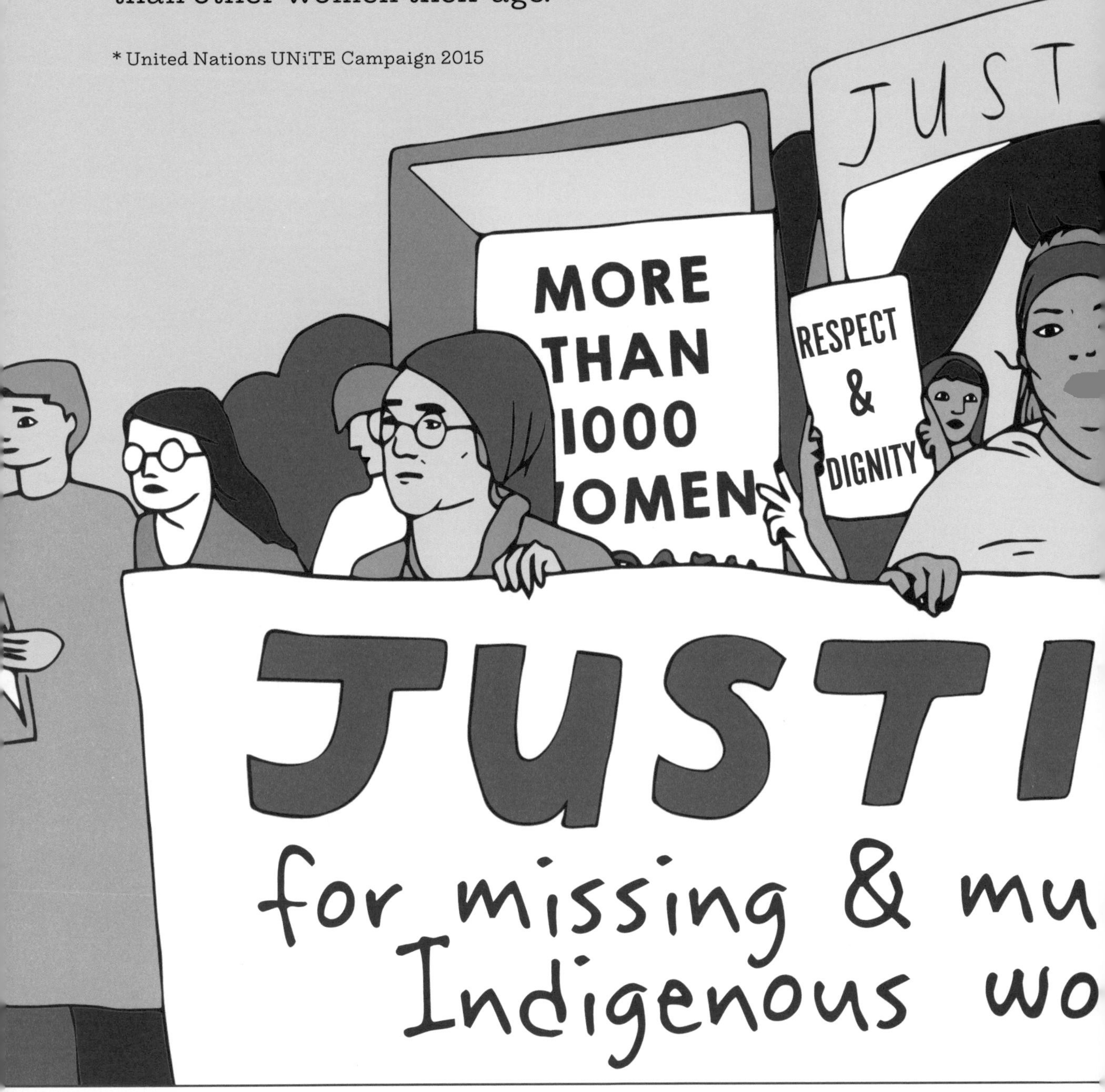
JUST
MORE THAN 1000 OMEN
RESPECT & DIGNITY
JUSTI
for missing & mu
Indigenous wo

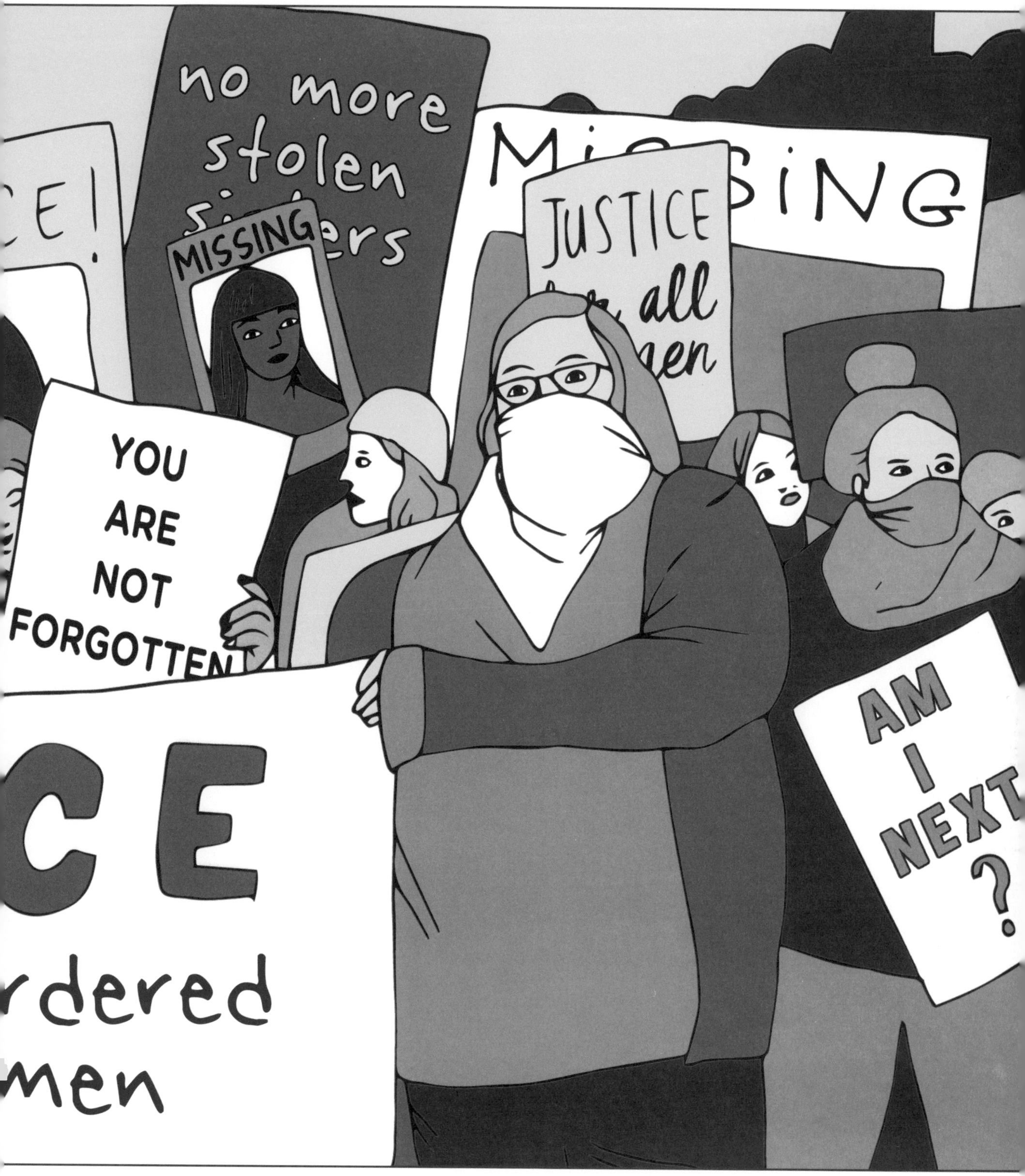
no more stolen
MISSING
JUSTICE
YOU ARE NOT FORGOTTEN
AM I NEXT?

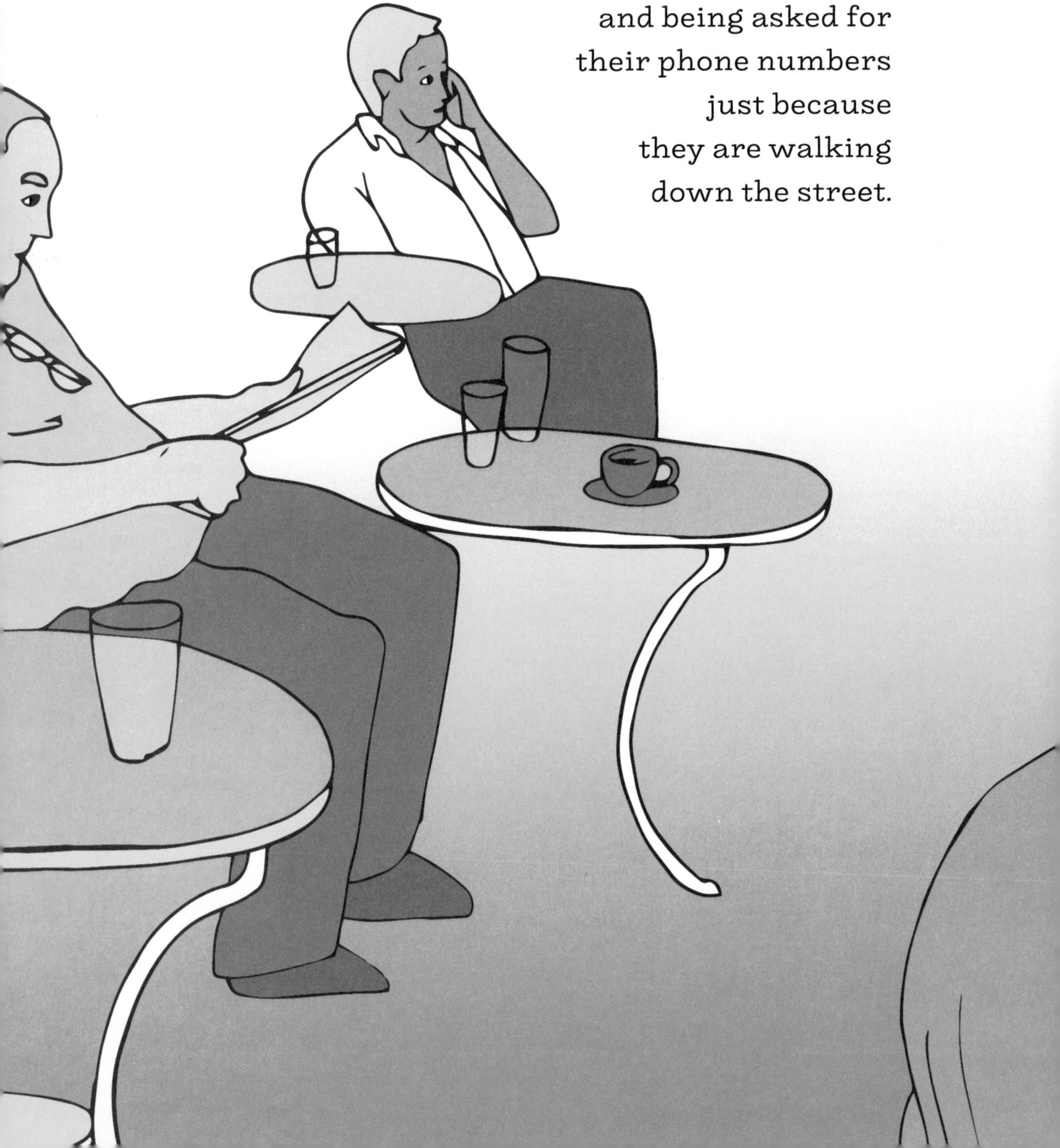

Girls are sick and tired
of being accosted,
of enduring catcalls,
and being asked for
their phone numbers
just because
they are walking
down the street.

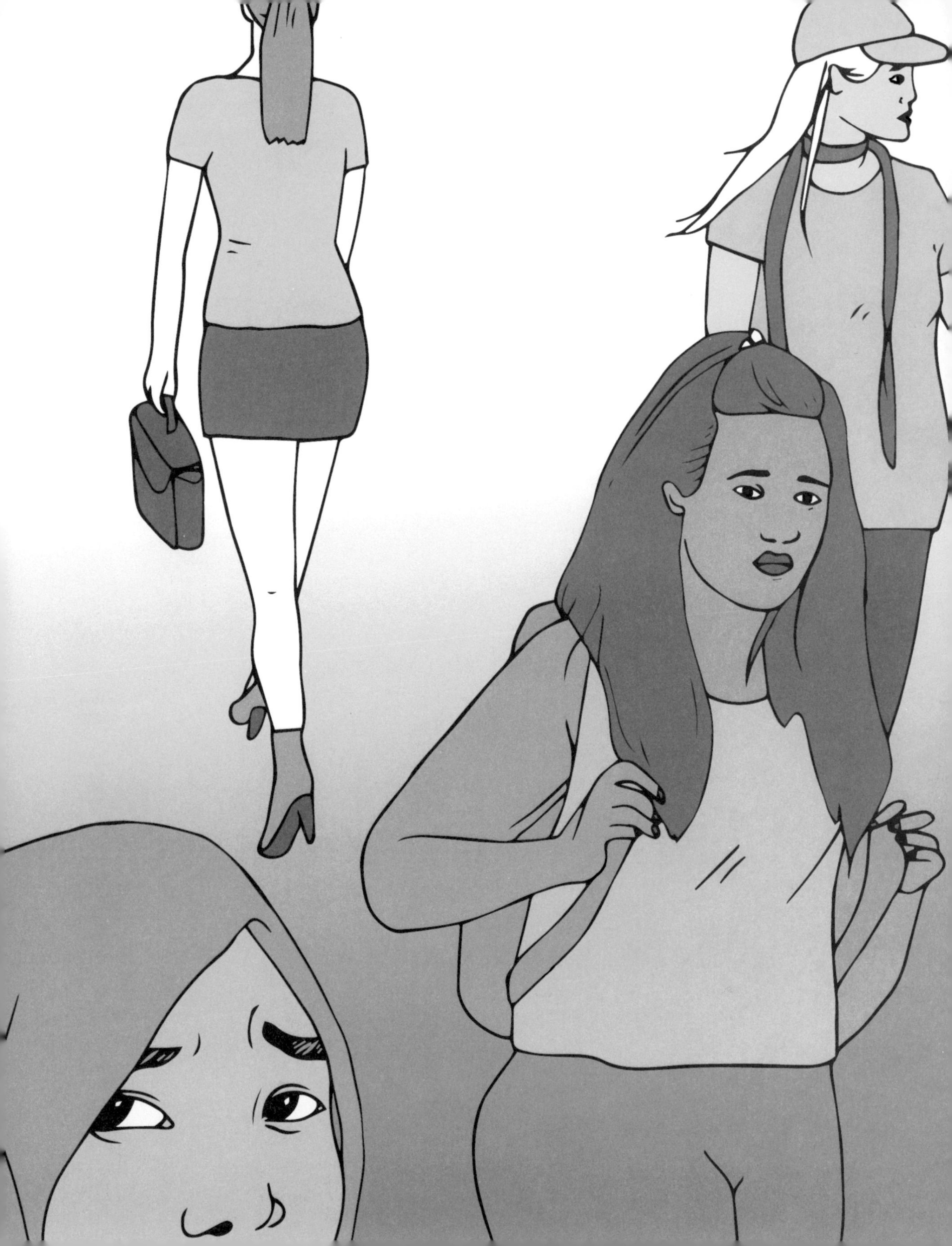

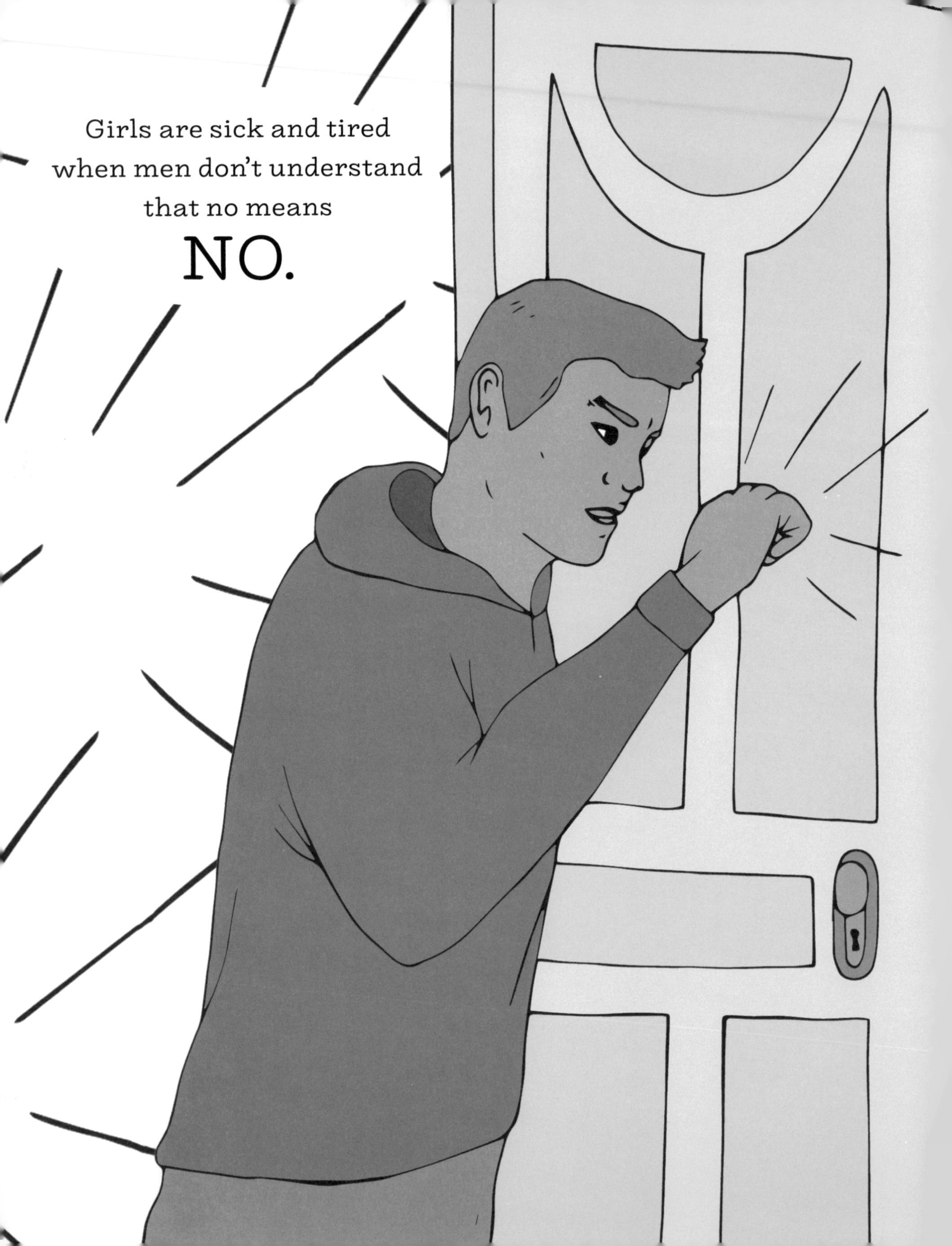
Girls are sick and tired
when men don't understand
that no means
NO.

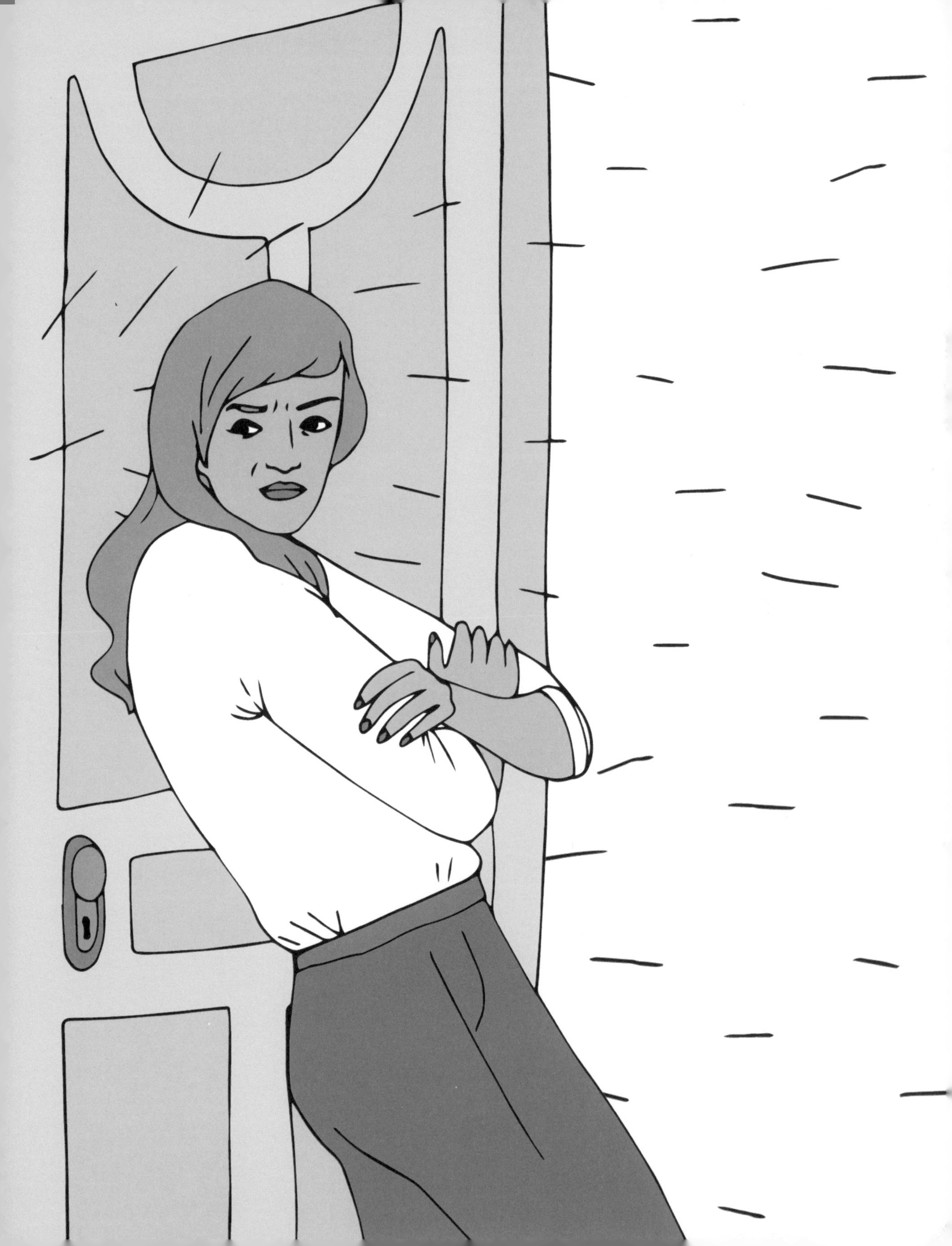

Girls are sick and tired when they report an assault and are treated as if they provoked it.

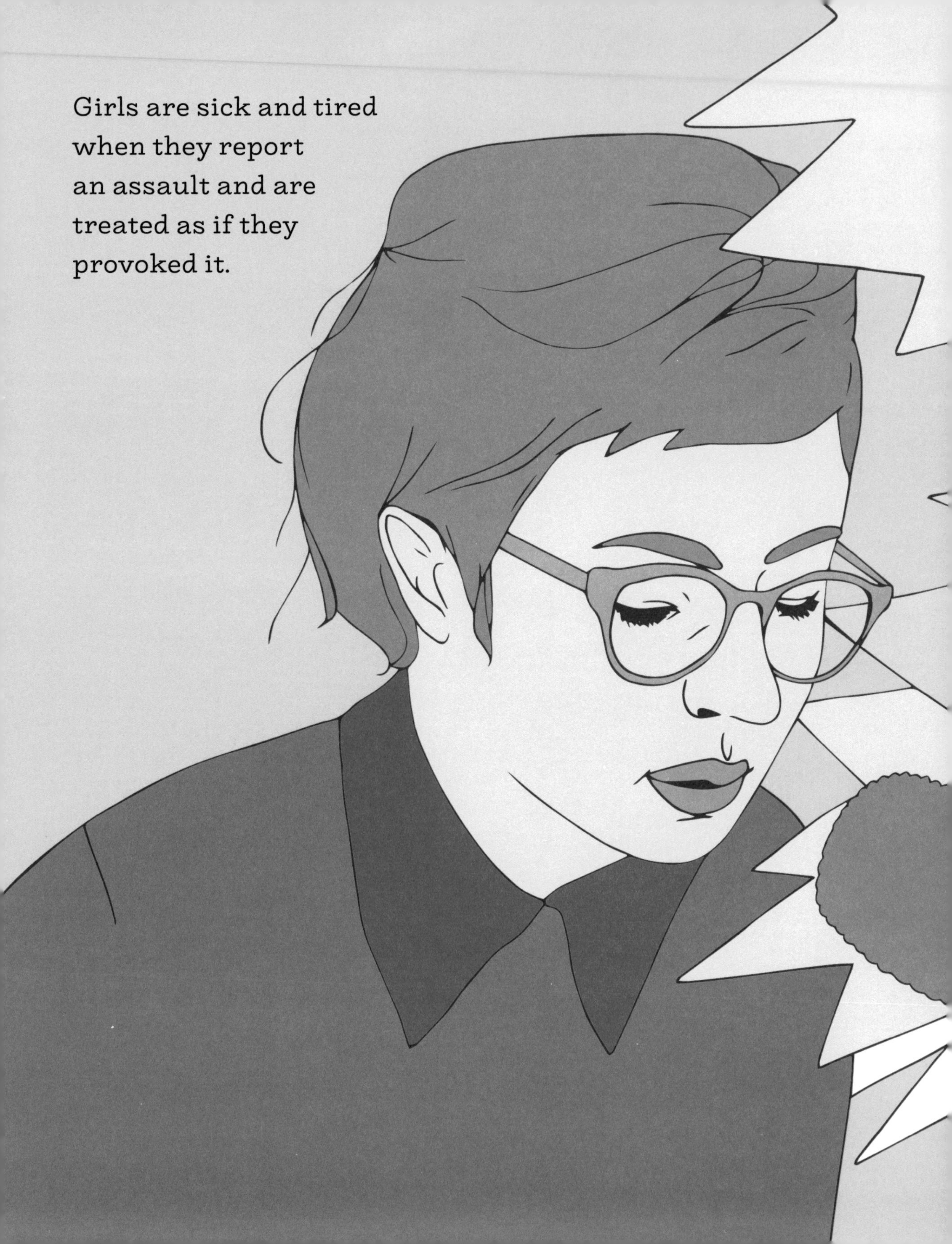

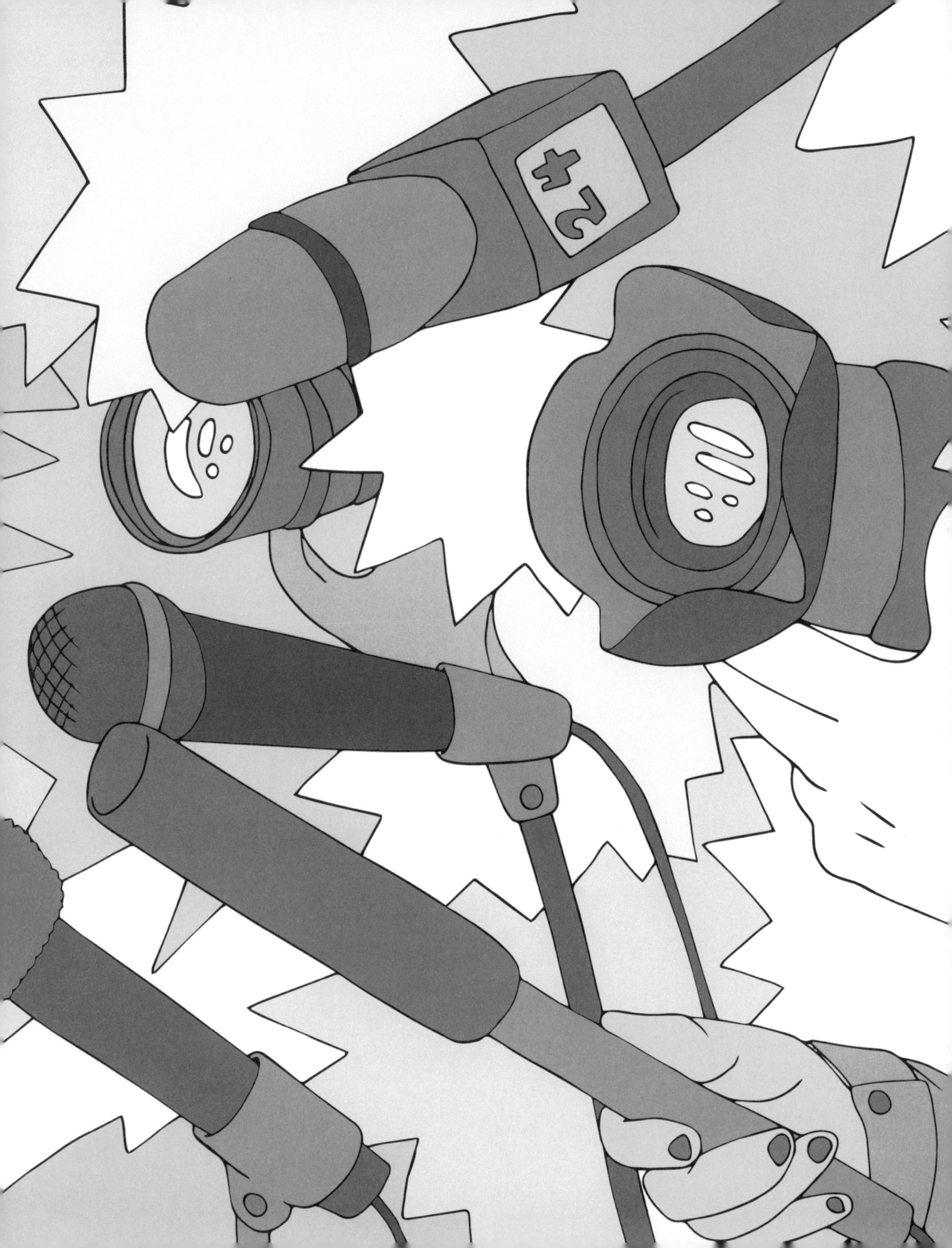
24

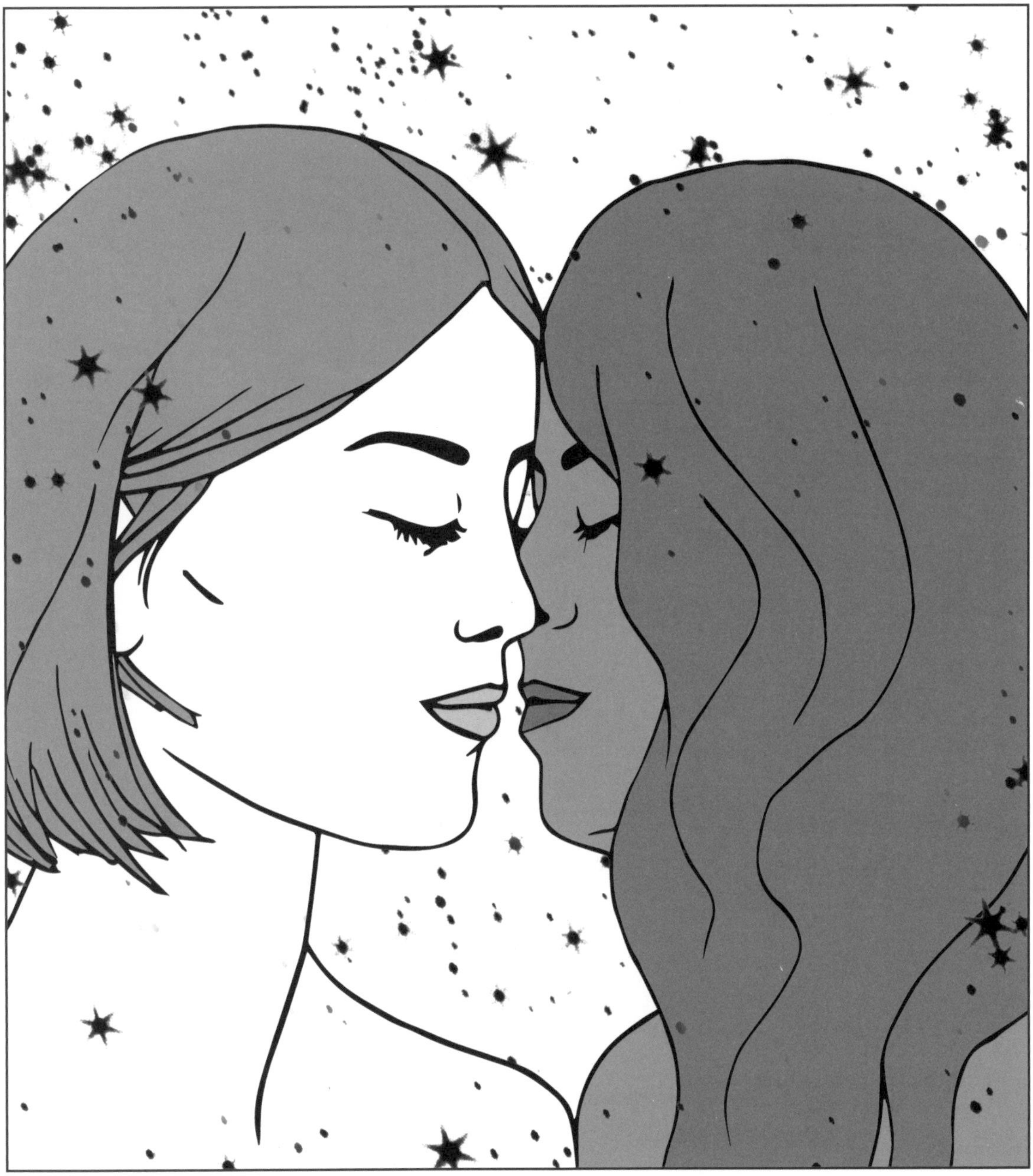

Lesbian girls are sick and tired
of serving as male fantasies.

Girls are sick and tired
when the word feminist
is used as an insult
and when they are
told they take things
"too personally" during
debates on feminism.

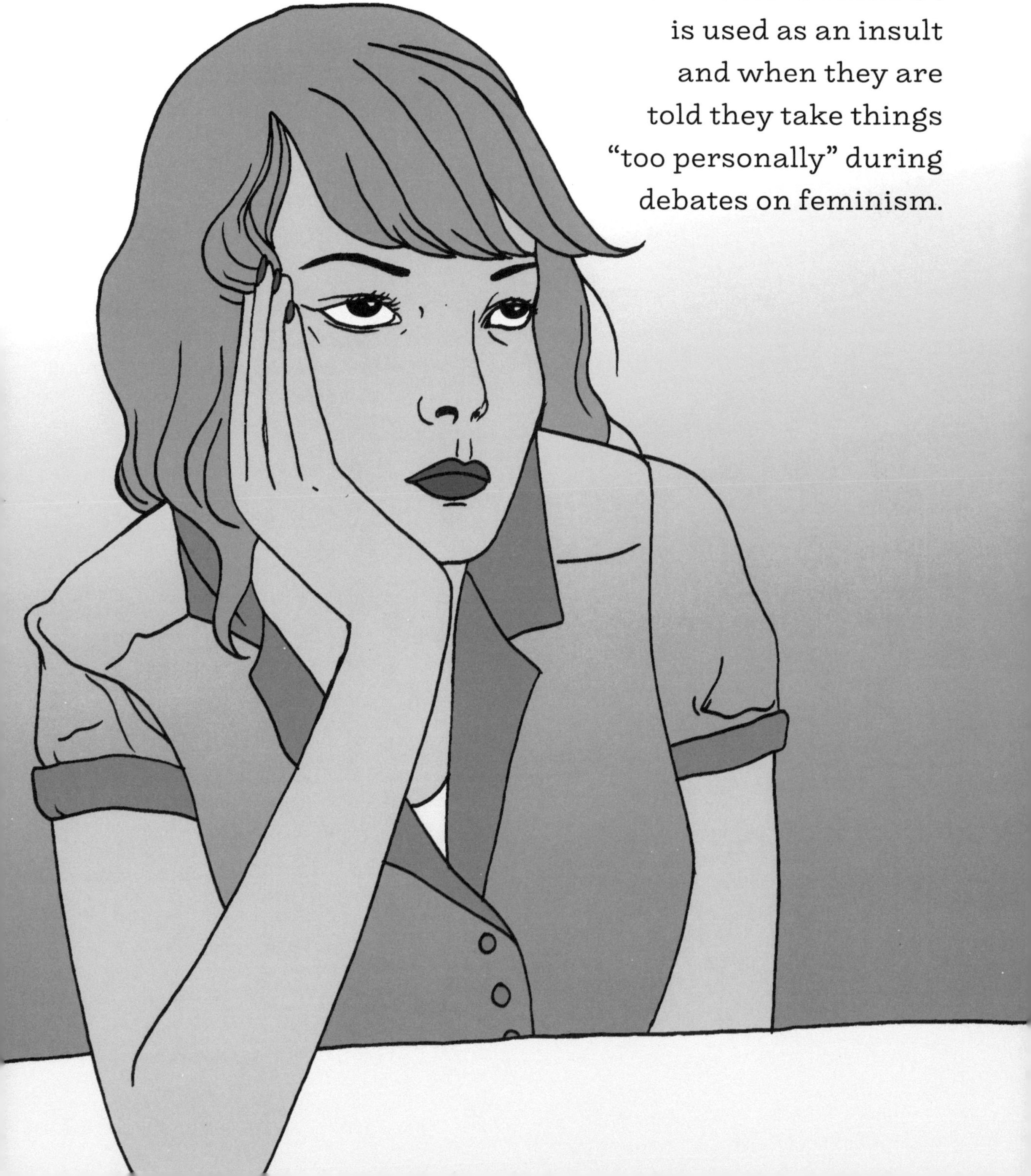

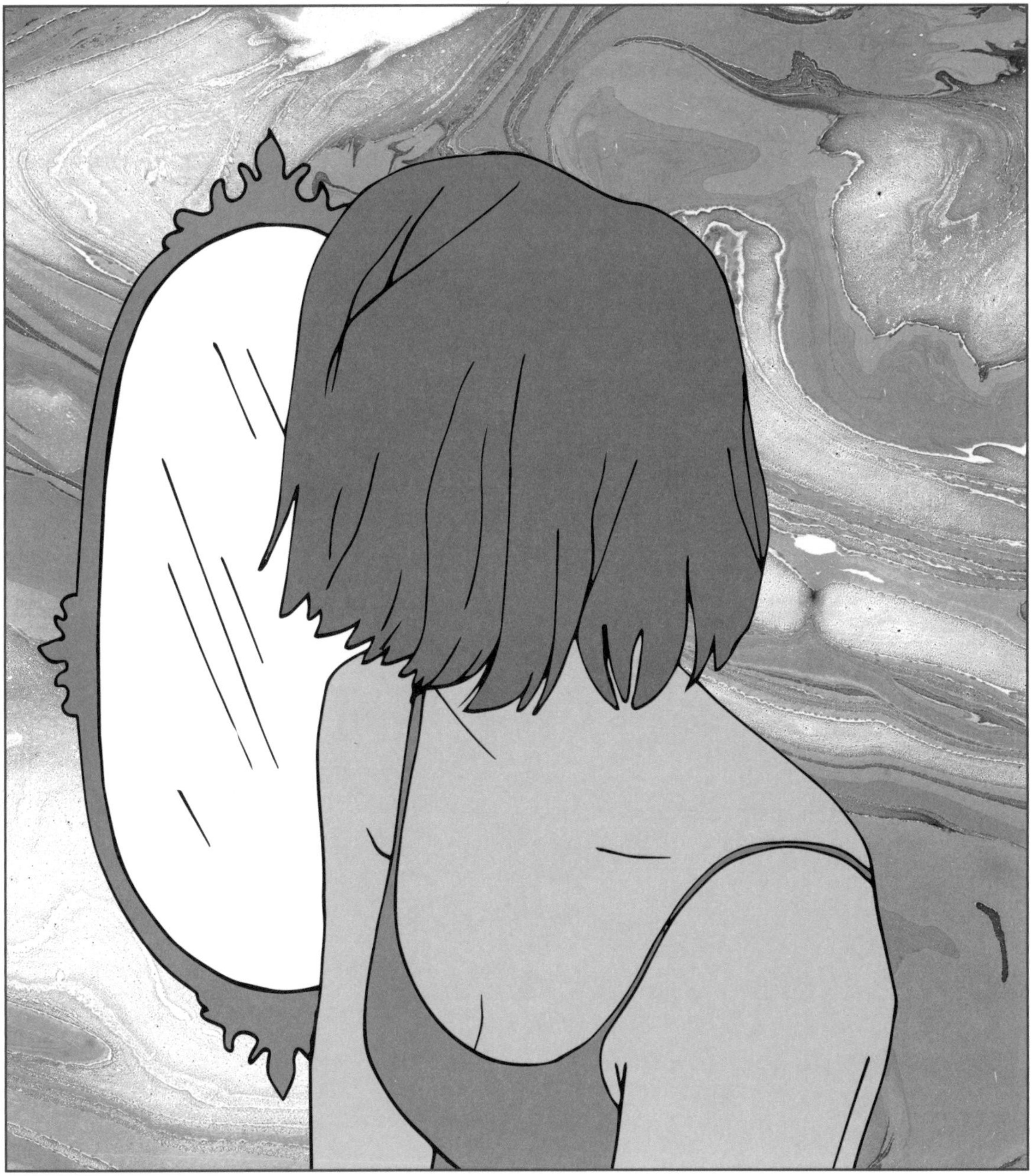

Girls are sick and tired of being asked if they have their period when something bothers them, makes them smile, or makes them cry.

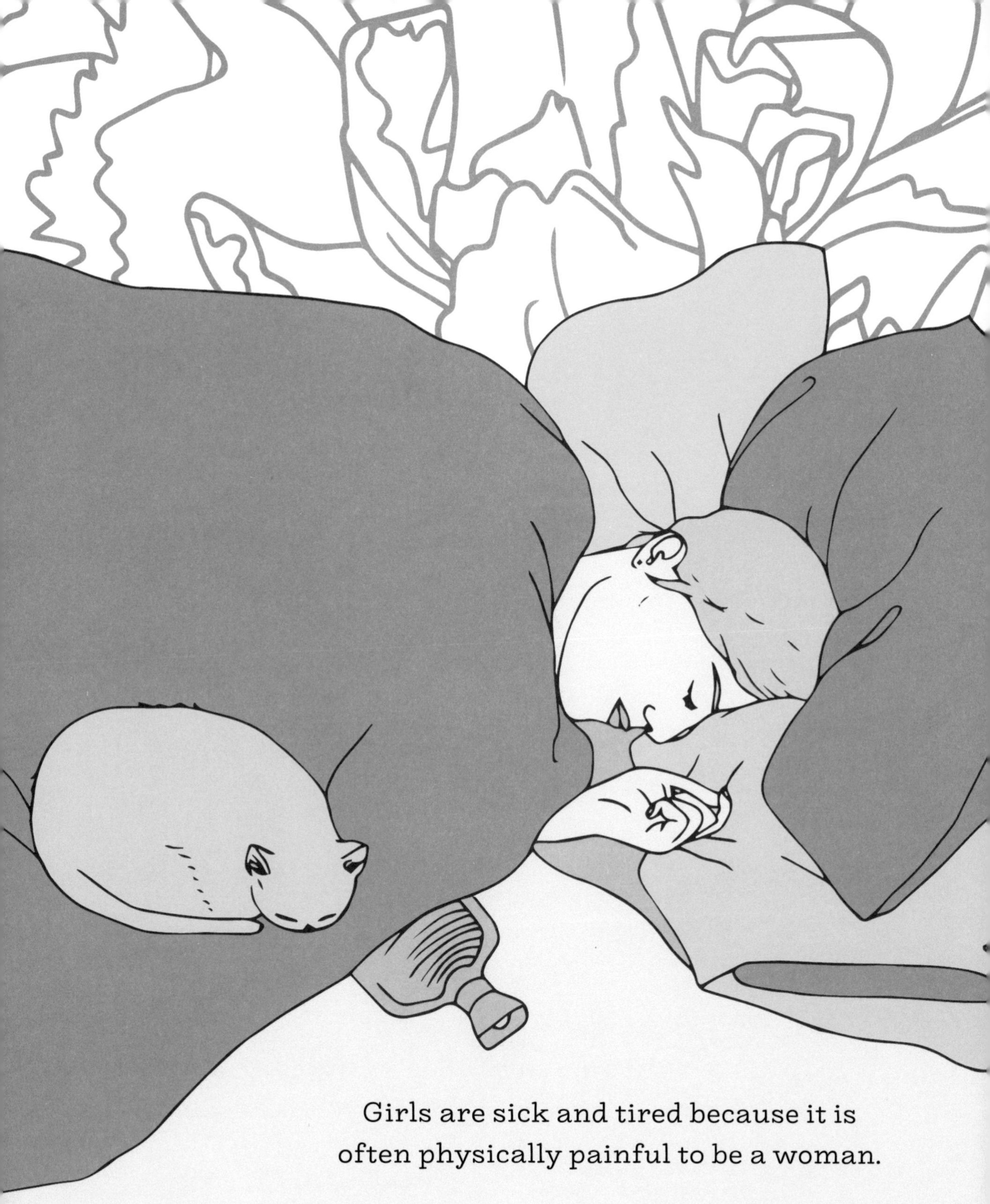

Girls are sick and tired because it is often physically painful to be a woman.

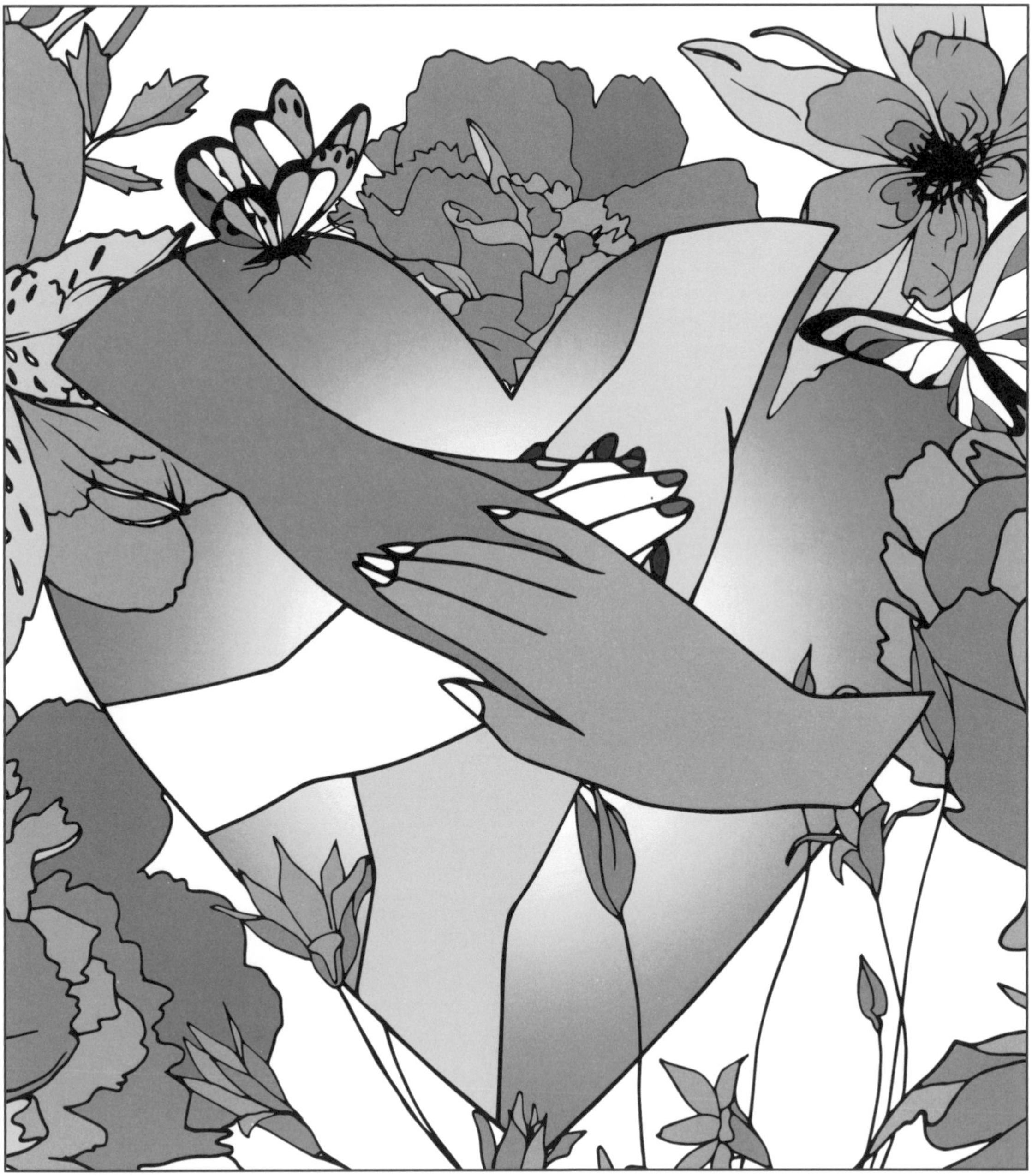

Girls are less sick and tired
when they are encouraging, supportive,
and united in solidarity with one another.

It's one of the best parts of feminism.

What Makes Girls Sick and Tired
was created to provoke discussion, reflection,
and action around feminism and the struggle
for women's rights. As privileged white women,
the author and illustrator are conscious that
their experience is far from being the experience
of all women. This book is therefore not a
complete description of all lived experiences,
but it hopes to offer a wake-up call to everyday
sexism and the other systems of oppression that
women and girls are subject to across the world.

Library and Archives Canada Cataloguing in Publication

Pesloüan, Lucile de, 1982-
[Pourquoi les filles ont mal au ventre. English]
What makes girls sick and tired / Lucile de Pesloüan ;
Geneviève Darling.

Translation of: Pourquoi les filles ont mal au ventre?
ISBN 978-1-77260-096-4 (softcover)

1. Feminism—Comic books, strips, etc. 2. Sexism—Comic
books, strips, etc. 3. Self-perception in women—Comic books,
strips, etc. 4. Women—Identity—Comic books, strips, etc.
5. Nonfiction comics. I. Darling, Geneviève, 1985-, illustrator
II. Title. III.Title: Pourquoi les filles ont mal au ventre. English

HQ1155.P4713 2019   305.42022'2   C2018-905953-2

Printed and bound in China

This English edition is an authorized translation and
licensed edition of *Pourquois les filles ont mal au ventre?*
© 2017 by les Éditions de l'Isatis, Montreal, QC

Second Story Press gratefully acknowledges the support
of the Ontario Arts Council and the Canada Council
for the Arts for our publishing program. We acknowledge
the financial support of the Government of Canada through
the Book Publishing Industry Development Program.

ONTARIO ARTS COUNCIL
CONSEIL DES ARTS DE L'ONTARIO
an Ontario government agency
un organisme du gouvernement de l'Ontario

Canada Council   Conseil des Arts
for the Arts   du Canada

Funded by the Government of Canada
Financé par le gouvernement du Canada | Canadä

Published by
Second Story Press
20 Maud Street, Suite 401
Toronto, Ontario, Canada
M5V 2M5
www.secondstorypress.ca